A Programmed Manual on Career Success

For People on the Autism Spectrum

Joseph Strayhorn, Jr., M.D.

Psychological Skills Press
Wexford, Pennsylvania

Published by Psychological Skills Press

Author's email: joestrayhorn@gmail.com

ISBN: 978-1-931773-24-9

Table of Contents

Chapter 1: The Goals of This Book..9
    To disclose or not...13
Chapter 2: The Five Most Essential Rules...15
    Appointment-keeping...15
    Sensory presentation...17
    Non-distressing behaviors..18
    Job competence...21
    Relations with bosses..22
Chapter 3: Some Unwritten Rules..24
    1. Don't neglect greeting and parting rituals....................................24
    2. Don't keep talking too long..26
    3. Think carefully before interrupting...27
    4. Think carefully before using CCC or T (commands, contradictions, criticisms, or threats)...27
    5. Don't talk very long about a topic the listener isn't interested in.....29
    6. Think carefully before changing the subject.................................30
    7. If you're interrupted, don't start all over when you resume...........30
    8. Don't speak too loudly or too softly...30
    9. Speak very distinctly..31
    10. Respect people's personal space...31
    11. Don't walk into people's offices without permission...................31
    12. Don't interrupt someone's flow of work too often.......................32
    13. Don't respond to things you overhear that weren't meant for you......32
    14. Be careful with certain topics of conversation...........................33
    15. Learn and use people's names...33
    16. Look at the other person's face some, but not too much..............34
    17. Don't look too long at attractive body parts other than the face......34
    18. Don't use curse words...34
    19. Cultivate at least one ally..35
    20. Don't make your down time obvious...35
Chapter 4: Emotional Regulation and Anger Control..37
    The most important thing to do when anger is high...........................37
    The goal in learning anger control, conflict-resolution, and emotional regulation.....38
    Practice figuring out what you're feeling, about what......................38
    Practice relaxation skills..41
    Influencing your feelings by choosing thoughts...............................44

The twelve thought system..45
The twelve thought exercise...47
The four thought exercise...48
Repetitive fantasy rehearsal with provocations.................................49
Alternatives to hostile or violent behavior.......................................50
Non-punitive sources of power..51
Chapter 5: Emotional Regulation, Part 2: Anxiety and Aversions.......54
Some aversions are good...54
SUD level...55
Mastery versus avoidance choice point..56
Internal sales pitch...56
Hierarchy...56
Habituation and desensitization...57
Exposure..57
Long-enough exposure..57
Self-talk...58
Fantasy rehearsal...58
Coping rehearsal..58
Mastery rehearsal..59
Fight or flight response...59
Breathe and relax...60
Mind-watching...60
Kindness to self and others meditation...61
Four-thought exercise...61
Self-discipline..62
PAST BAD and OH RAM PRISM..62
Summary: How to get over unrealistic fears and aversions................64
Chapter 6: Celebrating Your Strengths..66
Are you able to tolerate tasks others find boring?.............................66
Are you able to stay on task without being tempted to socialize?........66
Do you have a good memory for details?...67
Are you naturally honest?..67
Are you good at thinking outside the box in problem-solving?............67
Can you hyper-focus?...67
Are you good at math, physics, chemistry, computers, engineering.......68
The celebrations exercise...68
Two broad categories of things to celebrate: the two big goals............68
Categories of things to celebrate: The psychological skills list...........69

1. Productivity...69
2. Joyousness...69
3. Kindness...69
4. Honesty...69
5. Fortitude...70
6a. Good individual decisions...70
6b. Good joint decisions..70
7. Nonviolence..70
8. Respectful talk...70
9. Friendship-building...71
10. Self-discipline...71
11. Loyalty...71
12. Conservation...71
13. Self-care...71
14. Compliance...71
15. Positive fantasy rehearsal..71
16. Courage..71
Chapter 7: Social Conversation..73
The rhythm of social conversation...73
The one minute rule...74
Four ways of listening..75
Facilitations...75
Positive feedback...76
Follow up questions...76
Reflections...78
Putting telling and listening together: an example of social conversation.................81
Listening to criticism, especially from a supervisor......................................83
Chapter 8: Using Organization Skills..85
What should be organized?...85
Time and Tasks..86
Organizing stuff..88
Organizing papers...89
Organizing electronic messages..90
Organizing computer files...90
Organizing ideas..91
Chapter 9: Reading people's cues..92
Five ways that people send you messages...92
Tones of voice..92

Facial expressions..94
Gestures or body language...95
Try not to miss these messages..96
What if you're not sure?...96
Chapter 10: Improving the Emotional Climate.....................................98
The concept of emotional climate..98
Things to say to improve the emotional climate....................................99
Chapter 11: Decisions, Individual and Joint.......................................102
Optimizing versus satisficing -- what are the stakes?.........................103
Steps, or tasks, for individual decisions...104
   1. Situation. Understanding what is going on........................104
   2. Objectives..106
   3. Information..106
   4. Listing options..107
   5. Advantages and disadvantages...107
   6. Deciding..108
   7. Doing what you have decided...109
   8. Learning from the experience..109
   Mnemonic: SOIL ADDLE...109
Steps, or tasks, in joint decision-making: Dr. L.W. Aap....................110
   1. Defining the choice point..110
   2. Reflecting..111
   3. Listing options..111
   4. Waiting until listing is finished before evaluating..............111
   5. Advantages and Disadvantages...111
   6. Agreeing...112
   7. Politeness 112
   An example...112
   But people don't talk like this in real life............................114
Part 2: Choice points..115
   Schedule change...115
   Noisy cubicle..116
   Attention wanders after time...116
   Annoying lights...116
   Teasing perhaps?...117
   Simplified explanations..117
   Criticism from supervisor...117
   Deadline looks impossible..118

Work too easy...119
Coworker takes credit...119
Impending layoff..120
Uncertainty about your appraisal.......................................120
Disclose or not?...120
Chip in for baby?..121
Lunch together?...121
Irony from coworker..122
Did I make the person sad?...123
No allies...123
Not liking group chats..123
Empathy versus machine-talk...124
Topic is unfamiliar...124
Urge to repeat...124
Peer gives you jobs..124
Chain of command...125
"Would you mind?"..125
"Hate you" meaning you're awesome..................................125
Interrupt the presenter?..126
Start all over with explanation?...126
An imaginary kill...126
Change the topic?...127
Coworker's family member ill...127
Bosses are arguing...128
Minor correction..128
Correcting the emailer..129
Nervous smile...129
Unwanted job assignment...129
Wish to help criticized coworker.......................................130
Urge to keep questioning..130
Greeted but you don't know name......................................131
Discussion not directly relevant..131
Boss neither all good nor all bad.......................................132
Urge to moralize..132
Routines to be upset by move..133
Coworker catches on slowly..134
Boss criticizes part of your output.....................................135
Urge to correct, but new task..135

Puzzling idioms...135
Vague directions...136
Productivity unnoticed...136
Coworkers in recreational pursuits..137
What to wear...137
On task versus socializing...137
Fatigue from social interaction...138
The forest for the trees..138
You find yourself procrastinating..139
Focusing versus multitasking...140
Agenda temporarily empty...140
Increasing upset feelings...141
Your movements look unusual...141
Being efficient enough?..141
Dreaded retreat...142
Obstacle for project...142
Party isn't fun...143
Coworkers linger at lunch..143
Pressure to eat..144
Solution to overheard problem...144
Index...145

Chapter 1: The Goals of This Book

1. At the time of this writing, it appears that people whom statisticians count as being "on the autistic spectrum" have far less success in the workplace than their intellectual abilities would predict. But employers are recognizing more and more that this sizeable group of human beings collectively has assets to offer the workplace that should not be passed up. Some of the highest achievers in human history certainly had autistic-like difficulties with social interactions or sensory aversions. Albert Einstein, Isaac Newton, and W.A. Mozart all have been reported to have found social conversation either difficult or unpleasant.

What's the better summary of this text unit?

A. Isaac Newton was probably on the autistic spectrum.
or
B. The abilities of people on the autistic spectrum should be harnessed in workplaces with much more success than they are currently being harnessed.

2. If you are "on the spectrum," learning workplace skills can greatly add to your quality of life. Obviously, successful employment brings higher income. It also brings greater respect from people, and greater chances for success in relationships. And there is some evidence that having a job leads to greater life satisfaction, even among people who say that they dislike their jobs! Employment provides something that is even more important than enjoyable experiences: an "effort-payoff connection."

What's the better summary of this?

A. People on the spectrum have much to gain, in several different ways, by learning the skills for success at work.
or
B. It feels good to have one's own income and not to be supported by someone else.

What is the effort-payoff connection? It's knowing, or feeling, that what you do makes a difference in what sorts of good outcomes you get for yourself. Studies of both animals and people demonstrate that getting desired payoffs (or "reinforcers") contingent on what you do results in greater happiness than arrangements where your actions don't exert control over your payoffs.

Which of the following situations is an arrangment for more of an effort-payoff connection?

A. Someone wins a lottery and collects interest payments off the proceeds from then on.

or
B. Someone has a job as a coder and collects a paycheck in return for productivity.

3. Let's illustrate the effort-payoff connection by imagining three video games. Let's imagine that the object of all three games are nonviolent and cooperative: to make choices that prevent a disease from becoming an epidemic. In the first game, no matter what you do, the initial cases of the disease are successfully and quickly quarantined and treated and you have won. In the second, no matter what you do, the disease quickly spreads and becomes a terrible epidemic, and you lose. In the third, your choices make a difference, so that if you choose wisely, the epidemic ends, but if you choose impulsively, it spreads.

Which of these three games would have any chance of someone's enjoying it? If you say that the first two are "dead on arrival" and only the third would have a chance, then you appreciate the effort-payoff connection. The third is the only one with effort-payoff connection built in.

What's an important point that this text unit is meant to illustrate?

A. That video games represent a major industry, absorbing huge amounts of human labor.
or

B. It is usually more satisfying to achieve a goal through your efforts than to have the goal's outcome delivered for free.

4. The workplace is the prototypical arrangement for effort payoff connection: you do the work to the satisfaction of your employer, and you get in return a paycheck, as well as the prestige that comes from your career, the social contact of the workplace, the intellectual stimulation of the workplace challenges, and other payoffs.

Which of the following true statements is the author focusing on in the unit you just read?

A. Workplaces offer an opportunity for effort-payoff connection: you do your work, and you get money and other things as payoffs.
or
B. Throughout history, and into the present, many managers have failed to view the welfare of the workers as an important goal of the company, focusing instead on the "bottom line" of profits for owners.

5The purpose of this book is to teach you some ways to invest your workplace efforts, so as to get the most payoff. This book won't teach job skills such as nano-physics, computer programming, or cleaning up hotel rooms -- all of which entail specialized knowledge. But it does go into other general "workplace skills" that are often necessary no matter what the job is, including social skills, organization skills, and emotional regulation skills. Your success or failure in the workplace may depend at least as much on these skills than in knowing how to do the job in and of itself.

Which of the following true statements is the better summary of this text unit?

A. Even though different jobs require very different skills, there are certain skills that almost all jobs require: for example social skills, organization, emotional regulation. That's the set this book focuses on.
or
B. The author believes that the jobs that pay the least in our society often really contribute more important outcomes than those that pay the most, and that the honorableness and respectability of a job do not necessarily correspond to either pay or prestige.

6. What is autism? There is no foolproof method of diagnosing whatever autism is, or of saying exactly where someone falls on the "spectrum." The definition has changed greatly over the course of my professional lifetime. The people currently bearing that label differ tremendously among one another. If someone claims that "all autistic people" have a certain characteristic, different from other human beings, that person is almost certainly wrong. If I had to make

a generalization about autistic people, it would be something like the words of psychiatrist Harry Stack Sullivan, "We are all more nearly human than otherwise." A good fraction of what's written here is not specific to the Autism Spectrum, but just falls into the realm of "How to be a good employee," or "How to be successful at a career," period. So if you are not autistic or not sure, you're invited to keep reading and see if you pick up good tips for career success.

Which of the following better summarizes this text unit?

A. Scientists are working toward precise methods of diagnosing autism, in several different ways.
or
B. The label of autism has been applied to many individuals who are extremely different from one another, and thus it is difficult to make generalizations that apply to all people on the spectrum.

7. Despite the great variation among people labeled autistic, one thing most share is some perplexity, some difficulty understanding, or perhaps some lack of interest in, the "unwritten rules" of social interaction -- the stuff that people are supposed somehow to automatically pick up. Many people on the autistic spectrum find the details of physics or computer science easy compared to the art of human relations. And this is to some extent with good reason: the art of human

relations "is not rocket science" -- it's in many ways much more complex than rocket science! Human beings are much less predictable than inanimate objects! What many people automatically pick up, by what's called "incidental learning," others need to read about, consciously think about. One of purposes of this book is to make some of those unwritten rules written rules.

Which is the better summary of this text unit?

A. Social relations is a subject more complex and difficult than the physics of rockets.
or
B. If there is one characteristic most individuals on the autistic spectrum share, it may be that the unwritten rules of social interaction are not picked up easily by incidental learning, but require conscious study for mastery.

8. An important workplace skill is the art of social conversation. The "job interview" is a special form of social conversation. I have found that some people on the autistic spectrum can learn how to do social conversation quite well, if the different maneuvers in this activity are named, explained, and practiced one by one. One of the high-level steps in learning social conversation is learning to enjoy it thoroughly. If one acquires this ability, one has a source of pleasure for life, both on and off the job.

The author is here making a case for

A. Learning about alliances and political aspects of the workplace.
or
B. Learning to do social conversation well, and learning to enjoy it.

9. Many, but certainly not all, people who call themselves autistic share "sensory aversions": sensitivity to certain sensory experiences -- finding certain noises, lights, touches and smells aversive, much more so than most other people. One of the challenges on the workplace can be navigating around sources of very unpleasant feeling that are not unpleasant for others. Many non-autistic people also have very important sensory aversions!

What's an example of the sort of aversion discussed in this text unit?

A. Someone finds fluorescent lights very unpleasant, whereas incandescent lights are very tolerable.
or
B. Someone has an aversion to being criticized.

10. Many people with label of autistic spectrum disorder have difficulties with "emotional regulation" -- with staying calm in the face of events that may tend to cause intensely negative emotion. This is something that people on the spectrum share with vast numbers of people who

are not on the spectrum! In fact, skills of emotional regulation, in my opinion, should be taught to all human beings, if only we could be sure that this crucial skill would be taught well.

What's an example of someone's using the skill discussed in this unit?

A. A worker does a great job on a project and gets positive feedback, and is able to feel really good about this without discounting the approval he or she has received.
or
B. A worker discovers that a project he or she has put tremendous amounts of work into has to be completely redone. The worker is able to stay rational, decide what's best to do, and avoid loud displays of frustration.

11. How do I, your author, know anything about this? I'm a psychiatrist, and I've had the privilege of working with a good many autistic folks over the decades of my practice. I've also had many employees, and I've learned from their experiences what makes an employee a joy, or a sorrow, to have. And finally, I've been an employee of several organizations, and I've had ample opportunity to learn from my own mistakes and successes.

What's the purpose of this unit?

A. For the author to let you know the experiences that provide the sources for the advice given here.
or
B. To try to increase your motivation to study the art of workplace success every day.

To disclose or not

12. If you believe that you are a member of the set of folks on the autistic spectrum, should you tell your employer? On the one hand, the stigma attached to any label having to do with a mental health "disorder" has certainly not disappeared from the world. I can't guarantee that communicating a diagnosis won't result in discrimination against you. On the other hand, there are now legal protections provided to minimize such discrimination, for example in the USA by the Americans with Disabilities Act. Employers are being encouraged to actually seek out employees with "disabilities," including autism. And some corporations are taking it upon themselves to take advantage of what folks on the spectrum have to offer, and are making special efforts to make the workplace more user-friendly for such. There is more reason to disclose an autistic spectrum diagnosis than ever before.

What's the better summary of this unit?

A. The Americans with Disabilities Act applies to autism as well as a large number of other conditions.
or
B. There are pros and cons to telling employers and coworkers that you are on the autistic spectrum; over time, the advantages seem to be growing and the disadvantages decreasing; but you have to weigh the pros and cons for your particular situation.

Chapter 2: The Five Most Essential Rules

13. In the last chapter I said that human relations are complex. However, the most important workplace rules are fairly simple. This chapter names the most important things to do for career success.

1. **Appointmentology**. Show up when you're supposed to. Know what's second best to do when you can't show up on time.

2. **Sensory presentation**. Make a good enough sensory impression upon people. This means avoiding anything that says "not a good fit for this workplace" in what people see, hear, or smell when they encounter you.

3. **Non-distressing behaviors**. Don't do things that distress or scare people (especially, don't give any suggestion of a wish to hurt anyone).

You'll notice we haven't even mentioned yet anything having to do with carrying out the job the organization is paying you to do, or doing that job well. But here it comes:

4. **Job competence**. Do your job as well as you can, try to measure how effectively you're doing it, and keep putting energy into learning how to do it better -- without expecting perfection from yourself or anyone else!

But doing your job well is not enough.

5. **Relations with boss(es)**. Know which person or people evaluate your job performance, and furnish them the information to know you're doing it well. And while you're at it, be sure to treat this person or these people with friendliness and respect.

The rest of this chapter will go over these in more detail.

What's a summary of this text unit?

A. Be on time; think about how you look, smell, or sound; project good will rather than dangerousness; get really good at your job; cultivate good relations with your supervisors.
or
B. Develop alliances with co-workers; use devices to protect yourself from sensory aversions; think twice before attempting romances with co-workers; when in doubt about what you should do, ask questions.

Appointment-keeping

14. It has been said that "Eighty percent of life consists in showing up." Absenteeism and lateness are major

causes for employees to be fired. Here are nine rules of appointment-keeping:

1. Well over 95% of the time, simply keep appointments without changing them. Make the commitment to the time and keep it within a minute or two.

2. Know ahead of time whom you are supposed to notify if you discover that you can't keep a commitment to show up. Let this person know, as far ahead of time as possible. Try to minimize the chance that the person won't get the message: if necessary, leave it by text, and email, and voice mail, and whatever other communication means you have available.

3. If you can't keep the appointment with a person, see if you can reschedule for another time as soon as possible. If you can't show up on time for work or a meeting or can't complete work by a deadline, try to figure out when you can do these things and communicate them.

4. Try never, never to be a "no show," with no-showing defined as having someone expect you to show up in person or call at a certain time, and your simply leaving the person waiting. No-showing is the cardinal sin of appointmentology.

What is regarded as the worse example of appointment-keeping skills?

A. Telling a supervisor that a project is going to take more time than originally projected.
or
B. Promising to be somewhere or do something at a certain time, and just not doing it, with no prior explanation.

15. We continue with rules of appointmentology.

5. People are not perfect. If you should ever no-show, contact whomever you had the appointment with, as close as possible to the instant you have realized this. Apologize sincerely and reschedule. No-showing and then not being in contact is an even worse violation of good appointmentology than a simple no-show. If you no-show for a client, also let your supervisor know, and apologize to that person as well -- it's better that the supervisor find out from you than from the client.

6. If there is something you have scheduled that is outside your usual routine, and there is a chance you could forget, use the alarm clock function of your cell phone! Use technology to help yourself remember. Use of an alarm is a great aid to appointment-keeping.

7. The only way not to be late is to be early. If it's really important to be on time for something, plan to be a little early and plan something to do while you're waiting. But if you're really early, you

may want to wait somewhere where your presence won't be annoying.

8. The most honest excuse for lateness is, "I didn't start soon enough." Calculate how long things are going to take, and calculate when you should start.

9. What if someone shows up late or fails to show for an appointment with you? Now it's double standard time. You keep to yourself the lectures you give yourself about how important appointment-keeping is, and how an appointment is a promise. You want to be gracious and forgiving. You want not to be punitive or critical of the other person. This is your chance to show kindness and respect.

Which of the following is the worse example of appointmentology?

A. Being so early for an appointment that your presence in the waiting area distracts other people.
or
B. After forgetting an appointment, failing to contact the person to apologize and reschedule.

Sensory presentation

16. The second rule is: don't look, sound, or smell in such a way that broadcasts, "I don't fit with this job."
	Some jobs require people to dress a certain way, have their hair a certain length, not display piercings or tattoos, and so forth. If you're a lawyer, you had

better not show up in court wearing shorts and a tee shirt. On the other hand, if your work is to go into a room or cubicle by yourself and write computer code, it could be that no one cares what you look like -- but then again, they still might. How do you find out? One way is to ask -- for example you can get guidelines from a person in the personnel department whom you first talk with by phone, as to whether there is a formal or informal "dress code" for this job, and if so, what it is. When you're hired, you can ask your supervisor. The second way is to observe -- what do people at this workplace look like? Are there characteristics they all share? If they all dress a certain way, for example, you would at least form the hypothesis that supervisors want employees to dress that way.

What's a summary of this unit?

A. That you should wear the type of clothes to work that you would wear to a wedding or a funeral.
or
B. That you should find out what the written or unwritten rules are for what to look like at work, by asking and by observing.

17. With respect to sounds: when you speak, avoid speaking

too softly,
too loudly,

too indistinctly,
for too long without stopping.

Of all these, probably the most important is not to do anything more loudly than other people do. Don't laugh, hiccup, sneeze, groan, or make any other noise really loudly. In particular, do not raise your voice in anger -- don't ever yell at someone you're mad at.

The most important unwritten rule in the list above is:

A. Don't raise your voice in anger.
or
B. Don't speak too softly.

18. With respect to smells: aim for as little as possible. Remember that other people can smell your body odors more than you can. Be sure to wash yourself often enough. Avoid colognes or perfumes that give off a strong smell -- these trigger allergies in some people, migraines in others, and are not desirable for the workplace. The fairly mild smell that most deodorants have is fine, though.

Which smell is preferable?

A. That of an expensive perfume or cologne,
or
B. No smell at all.

Non-distressing behaviors

19. What employee behaviors are the quickest ticket to getting escorted off the property? The answer is: those that suggest the possibility of violence. This is particularly true in today's culture in which irrational mass killings make the news disturbingly often. If you are eccentric, different from other people, perceived as "weird," you want it to be clear to people that you are "nice weird" and not "dangerous weird."

What's the better summary?

A. It's very important that what you do and say lets people know you are of good will and not dangerous.
or
B. Irrational mass killings have increased greatly in recent decades.

20. Some folks on the autistic spectrum whom I've worked with find themselves automatically fashioning elaborate and sometimes very creative revenge fantasies concerning people who have crossed them. In the workplace, such fantasies should never be spoken aloud, nor written down in any form. The person having the fantasies may know that they would never be acted out, but other people may not be so sure.

It's important not to show anger in a loud and intense way, not to seem to be out of control, not to do things that are hostile or unkind, and not to say things that are insulting.

Suppose someone gets angry at a co-worker and imagines that a bomb would just happen to blow up the person's house. The advice is

A. To get the feelings of anger "out" by expressing the fantasy,
or
B. To be very careful not to communicate this fantasy in words or writing.

21. Some therapists try to convince people to "express their feelings," including their angry feelings. Sometimes such guidance does lots of harm. Expressing anger does not, as a general rule, tend to reduce anger, any more than expressing joy or cheerfulness makes you depressed. For the workplace, the less "aroused anger" you express, the better. This means: yelling, speaking very loudly, swearing, baring your teeth, getting in someone's face, banging on a table, standing up and moving closer to someone while disagreeing with them, are all NOT advised except in extremely rare circumstances. This advice doesn't mean you are helpless in the face of bad or aversive behaviors or incorrect ideas from other people. We'll talk later about how to disagree with people, how to solve conflicts, and how to ask people to change their behavior without being in a state of angry arousal.

When someone does something you don't like, the advice is to put first priority on

A. getting your feelings "out,"
or
B. acting like a reasonable and rational person?

22. Making loud displays of anger and hostility, especially while using swear words, and especially while making aggressive physical gestures -- these are the single quickest way to lose a job and spoil a career. Later in this book I'll go into ways of breaking habits of acting in this way. For anyone who has such habits, such work is absolutely crucial for job success.

At the time of this writing, there are plentiful models of insulting, disrespectful talk being broadcast to the public. One source is anonymous conversations that show up on the Internet. A second is political talk shows. A third is the talk among elected officials and those running for office, all the way up to the highest offices. You have to remind yourself that these models are not to be imitated in the workplace.

What's the better summary?

A. Despite many models in the media and in politics of what NOT to do, the desired workplace behavior is calm, polite, and in control.
or

B. Physical relaxation and fantasy rehearsal are two major techniques in learning anger control skills.

23. A second way of distressing people is by seeking a closer relationship with them than they want -- being too insistent or persistent in inviting them to be with you, to talk with you, to pay attention to you, to show friendship to you. In the era of the "me too movement," this particularly applies to males' invitations to females that the female interprets as having to do with sex. But one can be too pushy in attempting to foster even a platonic relationship. This advice is given with mixed feelings, because if everyone in the world were very afraid of committing a faux pas in this way, it would be a very lonely world indeed. But knowing when to back off, when to wait and see if the other person issues an invitation to you, and not pushing for a relationship faster than the other person wants, is a delicate art, but important one. We'll talk more about this later. But a conservative rule is: if you invite someone to do something with you, and the person does not accept, it's now the other person's turn to invite you. If they really want to get together, they know you're interested and can invite you if they in turn are interested.

What's the unwritten rule that is suggested here?

A. Watch carefully to notice the person's tone of voice and facial expression when you invite the person to do something.
or
B. If you invite the other person and they don't accept, consider it the other person's turn to either invite you, if they're interested, or not. If they don't invite you, don't push further.

24. Things are more complicated than this, because some invitations imply more closeness and intimacy and commitment to the relationship than others. For example, "We're going to lunch at the cafeteria now, if you'd like to come along with us," is a low-intimacy invitation; "How would you like to go to supper with me and then go dancing on Saturday night," is a higher intimacy invitation. You particularly want to avoid repeated invitations at the high intimacy end of the scale, with co-workers.

What's the complication that this unit speaks about?

A. Before inviting someone to do something that can be considered a "date," you want to find out if the person is already in a committed relationship.
or
B. Some invitations rank higher on the intimacy and closeness scale than others; the very low intimacy invitations are much less likely to be a problem than the high intimacy invitations.

Job competence

25. The most successful workers continually ask themselves, "How can I do this job better?" They read whatever they can that helps them answer this question. If there is a manual for employees, they don't just read it once -- they study it thoroughly. If there are revisions in the manual, they take careful note of them. If there are books and articles on how to do the job well, the successful worker does not passively wait for someone to assign these as required reading, but seeks them out and studies them carefully.

What's the better summary?

A. Keep asking yourself the question, "How can I do my job better?" and study whatever you can on that subject.
or
B. The Internet is now the best place to search for writings on how to do a given job most competently.

26. Some workers have the attitude that "I'm not going to work on job stuff on my own time. I'm not getting paid to do that." Such an attitude is a dangerous recipe for failure. In my own job, I have spent thousands of hours reading and studying about how to do it well, without getting paid anything for doing this, and in some cases paying dearly for this privilege.

In addition to reading and studying, you can learn from observing other workers and going to in-person trainings.

The writer's attitude is that

A. Workers should insist on being paid for the time they spend learning the important skills to improve their job performance.
or
B. Being extremely competent at your work is so important that it is a huge mistake to avoid trainings that you are not paid for.

27. Part of the job competence goal is learning more and more about how to measure your own competence. What are the outcomes that very competent performance of this job result in? How do you measure those outcomes? Are the outcomes you are producing getting better and better over time? Many workers probably never even raise those questions. If you keep them on your mind regularly, you will be more likely to succeed.

Which is the better summary?

A. You want to know how good job performance is measured, including the outcomes that good performance produces, and know how to measure your own job performance accurately.
or
B. A "process measure" refers to how the worker performs, for example does he or

she show up on time; an "outcome measure" refers to the quality of the worker's product, for example, if the worker writes a computer program, does it work well?

Relations with bosses

28. Jerry does magnificent work helping a group of co-workers on an important project. He comes up with the ideas that enable the project to be a success. But while devoting his energy to this, he neglects a less important project that his boss has assigned him. His boss doesn't bother to find out what he's been doing instead, and just notices that what he assigned Jerry to do hasn't been done. The boss concludes that Jerry is not a very efficient worker, and this is reflected in Jerry's job evaluation. The moral: to be a successful employee, you not only have to do good work; you also want to make sure that this fact is not lost upon your supervisors. Jerry could have benefited from a simple conversation, with his boss. Jerry might have said, "The group could really use my help on this, and I think I can contribute. It appears to me that this project is high enough priority that it might be worthwhile for us to put off the other project you gave me. What do you think?"

Which is the better summary of this unit?

A. It's not enough to do your job well -- you want to communicate well enough with your supervisor that your supervisor recognizes and appreciates your contributions.
or
B. Sometimes in the workplace you have to choose which is the highest priority way to devote your energy.

29. Sandra is writing a computer program. She is holding several complex processes in memory. Her boss comes up and stands beside her, waiting for a suitable moment to speak to her. She says, with some irritation, "Please go away! You're distracting me!" Other employees hear this remark. She does a wonderful job of writing the program. But her boss happens to be sensitive to disrespectful utterances, and is worried that Sandra will undermine the precedent of respect that exists with other employees. The boss seriously considers firing Sandra. The moral: Be aware of who has the capacity to: 1) fire you, 2) promote you, and 3) write your recommendation for the next job, and try to maintain very positive relations with that person or those people. Sandra would have been better off saying, "Could you give me just a few seconds, please, to write down a few things before I forget them ... OK, sorry to have to keep you waiting, but I didn't want to lose those ideas from memory."

Which is the better summary?

A. Be polite and respectful to your supervisors.

or

B. Prefacing a request or command with the word "Please" does not automatically mean that the directive comes off as courteous.

30. It's Tuesday, and Rolf gets an email from his boss -- the boss would like to talk with him for a few minutes, and asks what a good time would be. Rolf replies that Friday afternoon would be a good time for him. The boss is irritated that Rolf hasn't suggested an earlier time. Rolf would do well to make time for the conversation very soon, given that his boss is the one requesting it.

What's a summary of the unwritten rule stated here?

A. When your boss asks you to find a time to talk, find a time that is very soon.
or
B. When you are reading emails, it's good to recognize the ones that are of highest priority to respond to.

31. You want to be aware of the "chain of command" in your organization. It may be important to have a good relation not only with your boss, but also your boss's boss. However, sometimes if you go to your boss's boss about an issue, without keeping your boss in the loop, your boss may be offended about being left out.

　　In summary, you want to keep in mind that part of your job is to lead your boss to believe, (correctly) that you are 1)

a competent and productive worker, and 2) a pleasant person to be with.

What's a summary of the first paragraph?

A. Although it's good to have good relations with your boss's boss and those higher on the chain of command, when there's a problem or an accomplishment or any important news, it's best to tell your boss first, so your boss won't be embarrassed to hear about this from his or her boss rather than from you.
or
B. The phrase "chain of command" means that there are levels of authority in many business organizations, where people "report to," or are held accountable by, the person in the next higher level of authority.

Chapter 3: Some Unwritten Rules

32. This chapter continues the process of putting into words some of the rules and customs that employees are "just supposed to know," usually without ever having been taught them.

1. Don't neglect greeting and parting rituals.

Stan walks into the workplace in the morning, and Lou, a co-worker, says, "Hi Stan, good morning!" Stan thinks, "Yes, it is a good morning," and walks silently on. Without meaning to, Stan has just committed a social faux pas. He's broken an important unwritten rule: reciprocate when someone initiates a "greeting ritual" or "parting ritual" with you. If Stan had just said, "Good morning to you, Lou!" he would have created a social success experience, by participating in a "greeting ritual." The following words are often used in greeting rituals:

Hi
Hello
Good Morning
How are you
Good to see you
How are you doing?
Hey
Greetings
What's happening?
What have you been up to?

These are used not just at the beginning of the day, but when starting to interact with someone. Using the person's name along with the greeting ritual makes the greeting convey a lot more positivity. Importantly, if your tone of voice and facial expression convey enthusiasm and approval, these convey positivity too.

What's a summary of how to do a greeting ritual?

A. You just say "Hi," or something like that, in a friendly way, preferably using the person's name.
or
B. You make a series of very complicated decisions about which particular words to use when first seeing someone.

33. Similarly, the ends of interactions are often marked by parting rituals, using words like these:

Good bye
See you later
Nice talking with you
Thanks for doing this with me.
Have a good evening

If someone makes one of these parting statements to you, it's bad manners not to respond with a parting statement yourself, so as to complete the parting ritual. As with greeting rituals, using the person's name conveys more caring about the person.

What's a summary of this text unit?

A. If someone gives you a greeting, you should greet them back.
or
B. A parting ritual is something like "Good bye," said in a friendly way and preferably mentioning the person's name; it's good manners to reciprocate if someone gives a parting statement to you.

34. It's important to distinguish between a greeting ritual and a real request for information. The answer to "How're you doing?" as a greeting ritual usually is "Fine, how're you," or "Doing OK, thanks," and not a detailed report on how your life is really going. Similarly, the answer to "What's happening," is something like "Not much, how about you?" or "Things are pretty busy; how about you?" The message of such questions is, "I care enough about you to ask," but not, "I have allocated lots of time to listen to a detailed report."

Which is the better summary?

A. If in a greeting ritual, someone says, "How have you been doing," and you go into a detailed answer on the status of your life right now, you're mistaking a greeting ritual for a request for detailed information.
or

B. People can make a great deal of difference in how they come across, simply by doing enthusiastic, friendly greetings and partings with co-workers.

35. Imagine that two people encounter one another:

Jan: Hi Lee! Good morning to you!
Lee: Hi Jan! Good morning!
Jan: How's it been going for you?
Lee: It's been going well, thanks. How about you, Jan?
Jan: Doing just fine. Well, you have a great day.
Lee: Thanks! You too! Good seeing you!
Jan: You too, bye.
Lee: Bye.

Each person spoke 4 times, without their ever getting around to anything that someone might call "substantial." Why did they bother? Their conversation consists of nothing but greeting and parting rituals. Are they wasting their time? Not at all -- they are doing something important. Their greeting and parting rituals convey very important messages. Here's how they translate:

I care about you.
I want to be friends.
I wish the best for you.
There's a higher chance of our being allies (than there would be if we ignored each other).
There's a higher chance of either of us helping the other out.

There's the possibility of our having a longer conversation when we get the chance.

These are very important messages.

Which is the better summary?

A. It's quite useful to look at the other person's face when doing a greeting or parting ritual, so the person will be sure that they are the person you're talking to.
or
B. Even if a little social encounter consists of nothing but greeting and parting rituals, it accomplishes something: the people communicate that they care about each other.

2. Don't keep talking too long.

36. Each time you speak, you are making an unspoken request, or demand, of the persons you are speaking to. The request goes like this: "Please turn your attention away from whatever else you would be thinking about, and direct it to the thoughts I'm putting into words." People take turns taking "the floor" or "the microphone" -- they somehow figure out whose turn it is to talk at any given moment.

Many people on the autistic spectrum, as well as countless others not identified as such, have difficulties knowing when to stop talking and yield the floor to someone else.

When the author speaks about the floor or the microphone, he is referring

A. to literal objects.
or
B. to metaphors or symbols for the idea, "It is my turn to speak."

37. You may not have finished making your point. But you still need to stop periodically, so your listener can say, "Uh, huh. Tell me more," or somehow give you the signal that they want you to keep going.

How long is "too long?" It varies somewhat with respect to the type of situation -- a meeting, a lunch conversation, a conversation between two people passing in the hallway. But as a general rule, unless you are giving a lecture or a report, stop talking after at *most* one minute. Try to feel your time of having "the floor" gradually running out.

If you talk too long, people will often start sending you signals. They won't say, "Your time has expired; you need to yield the floor to someone else." They will look away from you. They may look at their watches or phones. They will look as though they are starting to talk. They may raise their eyebrows. Sooner or later they will interrupt you. If you want to avoid having to pay much attention to these signals, just pay attention to the clock inside your own head and stop soon enough.

At which time, in ordinary back and forth conversation, is it preferable to give the other person a turn to speak?

A. When the other person looks impatient, taps on the table, and then interrupts you,
or
B. When a minute or less has elapsed since you started talking?

3. Think carefully before interrupting.

38. If you watch political shows on television, you see people interrupting each other very frequently. Often two or more speakers are in a contest to see who can come off as most powerful. The viewers want to see a fight, and the speakers are fighting not only over the particular issue, but also over who gets to talk at any given time.

    Most people find it quite annoying to be interrupted. In the most productive and pleasant of dialogues, people take turns yielding the floor to each other without ever interrupting.

    The simplest rule about interrupting is, just don't do it. The more complicated rule is, interrupt only when someone has seriously violated the rule about not commanding the floor for too long. And even then, think even longer first, or just don't interrupt, if the person is your boss or your boss's boss or someone your boss is trying to impress.

Which is the better summary of this?

A. Expect that people will be annoyed to be interrupted, and do it only when you have a really good reason.
or
B. When you make requests of people, it is good to say please and to look at the person's face.

4. Think carefully before using CCC or T (commands, contradictions, criticisms, or threats).

39. There are four types of utterances that tend to antagonize people: commands, contradictions, criticisms, and threats. Here are some examples:

Commands:
    Leave that alone.
    Go away.
    Put that back there when you're through with it.
    Don't do it that way, do it this other way.

Contradictions:
    You're wrong on that.
    That's not right.
    You're mixed up about that.
    No, that's not the way to do that.
    Yes it is.
    No it isn't.

Criticisms:

Your code is too jumbled up.

Your plans aren't thought out well enough.

Why don't you do it the right way?

You don't know what you're doing.

Threats:

If you keep doing that, I'm going to make you wish you hadn't.

If you do that, I'm not going to work with you any more.

If you touch me I'm going to call the police.

What does CCCT stand for in this text unit?

A. Four utterances that create good feelings: compliments, commendations, comments, and thank-yous.
or
B. Four utterances that can antagonize: commands, criticisms, contradictions, and threats.

40. Sometimes the messages of CCCT need to be given, particularly if you are a supervisor. But there are tactful and tactless ways of sending these messages. The word "tactful" is an important one for workplaces. It means, "getting across your message in the way that is least likely to offend the other person." Let's look at some examples of how you translate messages from tactless to tactful:

Tactless command:

Get out of here; this conversation is not meant for you.
More tactful command:

How about I speak privately with Mr. Smith here for a few more minutes, and then I'll look you up and we can talk; OK?

Tactless command:

Quit talking so loudly. Quit distracting me.
More tactful command (now a request):

Excuse me, could I ask you a favor? I'm sensitive to noises; could you please move your conversation to a different place or speak a little more softly? I'd really appreciate it.

Tactless contradiction:

That's not right. You've got it all wrong.
More tactful contradiction:

My impression is that … (then says the correct idea without pointing out that the other person's idea was incorrect.)

Tactless criticism:

What you are writing is "spaghetti code."
More tactful criticism:

This code looks workable, but I have some suggestions as to how to make it easier to read and follow; would you like to hear them?

Tactless criticism:

    That's a stupid option.

More tactful criticism:

    A disadvantage of that option is that it would have a pretty good chance, I think, of resulting in:....

Tactless threat:

    If you don't start showing up on time, I'm going to suggest to our supervisor that you should be fired.

More tactful threat:

    Would you like to hear a concern I have? I'm worried that being late may be putting your job in jeopardy. I just felt obligated to say that, in hopes that it helps you out.

Tactless threat:

    If you launch this now, you're going to get your ass kicked.

More tactful threat:

    If you launch this now, I think you're going to be embarrassed by the bug reports that will be coming.

What's a summary of this text unit?

A. You just never should use commands, criticisms, contradictions, or threats.

or

B. If you send the messages of CCCT in very tactful ways, you can greatly reduce their tendency to antagonize people.

5. Don't talk very long about a topic the listener isn't interested in.

41. A very important maxim is: The fact that I find a topic interesting to talk about does not imply that someone else finds it interesting to listen to. You can directly ask people if they are interested in hearing about a topic. For example: "I've gotten interested in the topic of information storage media. Want to hear some of the things I've learned?" In most conversations, people are less explicit than that -- they say a sentence or two about the topic they're interested in, and pay attention to the other person's reactions. If the other person gives eye contact, raises the eyebrows, nods, says "Huh!" or even says, "Oh, tell me more," and otherwise looks interested, they go on talking some more. If the other person looks away, fidgets, doesn't reply, and looks bored, they cut that topic short right there.

Which is the better summary of this unit?

A. Make sure that when you keep talking about a topic, you're doing so not because you're interested in it, but because you have some evidence your listener is interested in it.

or

B. The two major outcomes that your social interactions are meant to foster are your own happiness and that of the others you are interacting with.

6. Think carefully before changing the subject.

42. When you change the subject in a discussion or conversation, you are making a command or request of your listeners, that if put into words would read like this: "Please stop thinking about what you're thinking about, and pay attention to something else of my choosing." If the current topic is beginning to get old, and you have predicted accurately that your listeners will find it more pleasant to think about the new topic, then changing the topic can come off successfully; when the opposite is true, changing the topic can be annoying.

Which is the better summary?

A. If you're not listening to what the other people are saying, it's hard to know how strongly they wish to stick to the topic they're on.
or
B. If you change the topic, do so because you think your listeners would like to move on to the new topic, not just because you would like to do so.

7. If you're interrupted, don't start all over when you resume.

43. Some folks have the urge to start all over; others don't. Sometimes starting back where you left off can be a good skill to employ. On the other hand, rather than just starting back where you left off, the interruption might be telling you, "We need to talk about something else instead." In this case, don't rigidly continue your speech, but listen for what the priorities are at this point in the conversation.

Which is the better summary?

A. Don't start all over again when you're interrupted, because the listeners will probably feel annoyed or impatient at having to listen to the same thing twice.
or
B. Don't interrupt other people, because they might feel the urge to start all over again.

8. Don't speak too loudly or too softly.

44. Your goal is to speak loudly enough that you can be easily understood, and that you sound confident, but not so loudly that you're irritating. If you consciously shoot for that happy medium, you're much more likely to find it.

Many of these unwritten rules, including this one, are corollaries of the same principle, namely:

A. When you speak or prepare to speak, think about the effect on the listener, not just about what you are saying.
or
B. Reflecting what you understood the other person to be saying gives you chances to clear up misunderstandings.

9. Speak very distinctly.

45. Remind yourself that the point of speaking is to be understood by your listeners, and you want to make it as easy as possible for them to understand you. You'll be easy to understand if you follow these two rules: first, say each word separately, with a tiny bit of silence in between each word. Second, put energy into the consonant sounds in the words: the p's, the b's, the t's, the s's, the f's, and so forth. If you make your consonant sounds very energetically, you can be understood well without speaking very loudly.

This unit advises you to put energy into pronouncing your

A. vowels
or
B. consonants?

10. Respect people's personal space.

46. Don't place any part of your body too close to someone else's face. About a meter away is the distance people often maintain when talking with each other at parties. The zone from about 6 inches to a foot and a half away from someone's face is the "intimate zone," and if you stick your face into that zone, it's usually very uncomfortable and often threatening unless you are the person's parent, lover, ophthalmologist, dentist, or are in a few other roles. The intimate zone is not for co-workers.

The part of other people's bodies you are advised not to get too close to is

A. the face,
or
B. the shoulder?

11. Don't walk into people's offices without permission.

47. When people have an office that is "their" room, get permission before walking through the door. This is usually true even if the door is open.

Knocking -- lightly, not too loudly -- on the person's door is a way of asking for permission to enter. If you catch the other person's eye and the other person motions for you to come in or says,

"Come in," of course you don't have to knock.

This suggestion has to do with the fact that

A. People like to be in possession of, and in charge of, their own "territory."
or
B. People like to think things through before making a decision.

12. Don't interrupt someone's flow of work too often.

48. It's good to ask questions when you aren't sure what to do. And it's fun to socialize with co-workers. But if your co-workers are doing things that require concentration, don't break their concentration by asking or telling them something more often than, say, once or twice in a morning and once or twice in an afternoon. On the other hand, if your job involves doing some physical job that you can do at the same time that you're talking, you can almost disregard this rule -- but not quite. It's still good not to direct someone's attention to you extremely often.

One logical reason for the advice given in this unit is that

A. People often are feeling time pressure to get something finished, and an interruption slows down the progress toward their goal.
or
B. People don't like to share personal details with people until they have had a chance to get to know the person and share less personal pieces of information.

13. Don't respond to things you overhear that weren't meant for you.

49. Tom is seated in the lunchroom, and he overhears two people speaking to each other at a table behind him. One of the two people says, to the other,"I'm trying to remember the name of that television series about the robots that developed consciousness, where there was a beautiful robot of an Asian lady named Mia..." Tom turns around and says, "The series was called 'Humans.'" Tom feels that he is just being helpful -- after all, the person said he was trying to remember, and Tom furnished the right answer. When he gets a less than friendly reaction, he wonders what he did wrong. What he did wrong was responding to something someone said to someone else, in what was meant to be a private conversation. Even if people overhear private conversations, they are supposed to pretend they didn't hear!

The more private and personal the subject matter is, the more important this rule is. Suppose in the same situation, one of the two people had said to the other,

"My wife just doesn't seem to be as friendly to me as she was. I'm not sure what to make of it." If Tom had turned around and said, "Why don't you just ask her what's going on?" this would have been a much bigger faux pas.

What's a major idea of this section?

A. Remembering trivia about television series is something some people value more highly than others do.
or
B. Sometimes when you overhear people speaking to each other, in crowded quarters, you should act as if you don't hear, so as to give the people the sensation of privacy.

14. Be careful with certain topics of conversation.

50. Here are some topics of conversation to be careful about: sex, religion, politics, people's finances, which people you or someone else dislikes, people's ethnicity, people's body parts, your own feelings of sexual attraction to a co-worker, and things you don't like about people. You don't have to avoid these altogether, forever. Rather, you want to wait until you've gotten to know someone, and you have some knowledge about what's likely to offend the person and what isn't.

Topics like the weather, sports contests, video games, computer systems, cars, planes, other machines, music, how to do the job well, getting to and from work, food, pets, events in the news

(without editorial comment, if you're in a different polititcal tribe from the other person), and things you like about people are less likely to evoke any strong negative feelings. Regardless of this, keep in mind suggestion #5 above, and gauge your listener's interest in the topic before talking too long about it.

Which topic of the following two is less likely to offend someone?

A. Which of two races of people they find more attractive.
or
B. How much memory in a computer is necessary, and how much is a waste of money.

15. Learn and use people's names.

51. Taking the trouble to know someone's name is the most elementary way to say, "I care about you." Greeting and parting rituals are a great circumstance to address the person by name.
Why do you think this advice is given?

A. Because the fact that you know the person's name tells that you care enough to remember, first of all, and because your mentioning their name shows you are thinking about whom you are talking to.
or
B. Because people are grateful when you help them out with something that makes life easier for them.

16. Look at the other person's face some, but not too much.

52. Much is made of people's habits of "eye contact." Unless you are very close to someone, the person can't tell whether your eyes are focused on their eyes, their nose, or their mouth. If you never look at their faces, people seem to feel that you are avoiding connecting with them, and they don't like it. If you maintain a fixed stare at their faces, they often feel that you are being too intense. So the thing to do is look at the person's face for a few seconds, look away for a few seconds, and keep alternating. It isn't horrible to break this rule. But following it does make people more comfortable with you.

Which is the better summary?

A. Always make eye contact.
or
B. Look at the person's face for some of the time when you are speaking and listening, and look away for another part of the time, so that you are connecting, but not staring.

17. Don't look too long at attractive body parts other than the face.

53. For example: don't stare at a woman's breasts or legs, especially if you're not very far away from her. (From what we've learned in high school geometry, the closer you are, the more obvious it is which body part your eyes are glancing at -- or staring at -- because the angle of your eyes or head is greater). People want to be attractive, but they get "creeped out" if people enjoy their attractiveness too much or in the wrong circumstances.

Which is the better summary?

A. If you find someone sexually attractive, try not to make that fact obvious by the direction of your gaze.
or
B. You are not supposed to find co-workers attractive.

18. Don't use curse words.

54. When can you get away with using the words, "God damn it," without antagonizing someone? How about the word "fuck?" Or the phrase "mother fucker?" The answers to these questions depend upon the situation, the listeners, the particular way the words are used, and still other factors. The social calculations are often quite complex. I

recommend sparing yourself the complexity of all this: in the workplace, just don't ever use the common "taboo words" that people find offensive. There are other ways to get any point across.

The same general advice goes for jokes that can be offensive because of crossing the line into bad taste because of sexual, racial, or macabre elements. In the workplace, it's better to be safe than sorry. To a first approximation, just skip them.

The advice is to

A. Think about the number of times you have heard your listener use swear words before using them yourself; also think about each of the other listeners; also think about the context of the conversation.
or
B. Just make things simple for yourself by avoiding using taboo swear words altogether.

19. Cultivate at least one ally.

55. It's great to get to know at least one co-worker other than your supervisor. You and this person can ask and answer questions when you're not sure of something, and can help each other out in other ways. One of many positive results is that you don't have to bug your supervisor too often.

What's a summary?

A. "Network" with at least one co-worker at your own level, for mutual support.
or
B. Supervisors would rather have you ask questions than to do something wrong.

20. Don't make your down time obvious.

56. What do people do at work when they have finished a task, no new one has been assigned, and they don't have the opportunity to get assigned or figure out a new task? Sometimes they fall asleep, play video games, surf the internet, watch the news, chat with co-workers -- in other words, goof off. But employers and supervisors usually have an aversion to paying people to goof off. They mind it even more if someone does it in an obvious way, because this tends to set the precedent that other workers are welcome to do the same thing. So for this reason, I recommend using your "down time" to organize your materials, read manuals on how to do your work well, revise your filing system, get rid of to do list items that can be done at any time, check work that has already been done, and so forth.

If you understand your job and its mission well enough, efforts to "look busy" will usually be unnecessary, because you'll know in advance the next steps on the to do list once the current one is finished.

What is this unit advising against?

A. Goofing off or resting for very long in a very obvious way, unless you know it's permitted and encouraged.
or
B. Trying to understand too much about everyone else's job and the total mission of the organization rather than focusing on your own tasks?

Chapter 4: Emotional Regulation and Anger Control

57. As we've discussed already, being able to stay cool and calm is one of the most important job skills. Put another way, getting so angry or upset that you yell and seem to "go out of control" and make people worry that you will do something harmful is probably the quickest way to lose a job.

One of the goals for the skill of emotional regulation is simply to avoid ever raising the voice in anger while in the workplace. Your first priority is coming across as a reasonable person, and not "getting your feelings out." Does this mean that "bottling up" anger is better than "letting it out?" If you're only given a choice between these two, it sure does! This is true despite much that has been written in pop psychological self-help books! However, there are other options. One of the major accomplishments of cognitive therapy is refining techniques of not working up unwanted degrees of anger in the first place. One of those techniqes is seeing anger not as a "thing" that you keep in or let out, but a set of behaviors that you can to a large extent choose to do or not to do.

The author implies that in situations that get you angry, the most important thing to do is
A. To figure out a reasonable thing to do,

or
B. to get the anger "out"?

The most important thing to do when anger is high

58. What's the highest priority if you have gotten really angry, or someone has gotten really angry at you? It's not to get feelings out, to teach the othe person a lesson, or get revenge. It's not even solving the problem that caused the anger. It's preventing any violence or permanent harm to relationships. Usually the best way to do this is putting physical distance between yourself and that person until you have both cooled off. That is, try to excuse yourself politely and walk away, to a different room from that person, some place out of sight, out of hearing. Talking the problem out can wait until both people are fairly calm. People don't do good problem-solving when they're very angry. They tend to look at every statement the other person makes as something to dispute or prove wrong. I'm convinced that if everyone in the world followed the advice in just this paragraph, the world's rates of murder and assault would plummet.

What's a summary of the advice in this unit?

A. Practice trying to see things from the other person's point of view and to realize how the other person is feeling.
or
B. When anger is really high, move away from the other person and let both of you cool off.

The goal in learning anger control, conflict-resolution, and emotional regulation

59. In order to express the goal, let's define the word "provocation." A provocation is any situation that might bring out anger or distress. Someone steps on your foot, someone criticizes you, someone spills water on you, you get "killed" in a video game -- the number of possible provocations is almost infinite. The goal is to come up with the best possible response, or at least a good response, to provocations -- to handle provocations by making good choices.

But what do we mean by a "good" choice? It's a response that tends to cause the most of 1) your own long-term happiness, and 2) the long-term happiness of the people you affect.

This text unit defined

A. a provocation, and a good response to provocation?
or
B. the difference between anger and irritation?

Practice figuring out what you're feeling, about what

60. Emotions are very important signals to us. For example, when we feel scared, our brains are signaling to us that we may be in some danger that we may need to protect ourselves from. Is there really danger, or is our brain giving us a false alarm? If there is danger, what is it, and what, if anything, can we do to protect ourselves from it? The answers to these questions can literally make the difference between life and death, and this is why the capacity to feel fear evolved in the first place.

The attitude toward fear that is expressed in this text unit is that

A. Fear can be a very important signal that danger is present; this signal can be life-saving.
or
B. There are several ways of reducing fear that is unwanted or unrealistic, and almost all these involve practicing with the scary situation in some way.

For another example, when we feel guilty, our brains are signaling to us that we have done something wrong, something we shouldn't have done. Again: are we getting a false alarm, or have we really done something wrong? If we have, what is it, and what can we do about it (either to make amends, or to make sure we don't do it again)?

For a third example: when we feel angry, our brains are signaling to us that someone else has done or is doing something undesirable or dangerous to us, something that we may need to defend ourselves against. Again: are we getting a false alarm, or is someone really harming or about to harm us? If someone is doing something unwanted to us, what do we want to do about that?

For a fourth example: when we feel curious, our brains are signaling to us that there is something worth finding out or learning about. What is it, and how do we want to find out more about it?

This text unit makes what point about emotions?

A. Emotions give us important signals and clues about what sort of situation we're in and how we should respond.
or
B. The limbic system of the brain and the sympathetic nervous system are very much involved with emotions.

61. There are a good number of "feeling words." Here are a few to be familiar with:

Pleasant feelings:

fun
liking
interested
lighthearted
proud
happy
grateful
blessed
compassionate, sympathetic
curious
enthusiastic
relieved
determined, motivated
confident

Unpleasant feelings:

sad
scared (worried, frightened, anxious)
guilty
ashamed, embarrassed
angry
disliking, hating
frustrated
disgusted
regretful
demoralized, hopeless
distressed, upset, disturbed
trapped

Can be pleasant or unpleasant

energized
tired
surprised

Why do you think the author lists these words?

A. Because they summarize in one word some mental processes that are very useful to be aware of, both in oneself and others.
or
B. Because they are useful in writing any sorts of stories.

62. Can you remember a time when you have felt each of these ways? For many people on the autistic spectrum, (and as usual, for many other people too) these words are rather unfamiliar, and the question, "When have you felt this emotion:____," is very difficult to answer. Here's an even harder question: for each of these emotions, when was a time when you recognized that someone else was feeling that way? (Examples from books or movies or news reports, as well as real life, are just fine.)

What is a quick summary of the two questions the author, through this text unit, suggests asking yourself?

A. How am I feeling, and how are other people feeling?
or
B. What's at stake, and how big are the stakes?

63. If you make a project of paying attention to emotions, you can gradually expand your sensitivity to them and your accuracy in perceiving them. Ask yourself:

What's the emotion?
What situation triggered it?
Was it a false alarm, or was there a really good reason to feel that way?
How did I or someone else respond to this situation?
What do I think would have been the best response to that situation?

The author, in this text unit, advises

A. Paying attention to emotions, the situations that trigger them, and the responses to them.
or
B. When in doubt, acting kindly?

64. How does asking yourself these questions help with "emotional regulation" and "staying cool?" The more you can use words and language to think about emotions, the situations that elicit them, and the responses to those situations, the more you are able to think rationally about all that, so as to make better decisions. Rational decision-making is the opposite of losing control and having an outburst that harms you. Also, when you practice recognizing feelings, especially anger, you can start deciding what to do about the situation early, before the anger builds up to the point that it hampers your ability to decide well.

The major point of this text unit is that

A. Being able to speak (to yourself or others) articulately about situations involving emotions helps you to make rational and reasonable decisions.
or
B. Many psychologists consider emotions to be behaviors that can be increased or decreased by the consequences they bring about.

Practice relaxation skills

65. When people lose their tempers, they almost always have a high degree of activity in their "sympathetic nervous systems." This term doesn't have anything to do with sympathy. It's the word someone gave to the part of the human nervous system that prepares for "flight or fight." This part of the nervous system turns up the muscle tone (makes the muscles more tense), turns up the heart rate, turns up the rate of breathing, increases sweating, constricts the small blood vessels, and increases blood pressure. The tendency toward calm, cool, and unhurried decision-making tends to go down. Importantly, feeling very relaxed and peaceful usually means low sympathetic nervous system activity.

What's a summary of what the sympathetic nervous system does?

A. It gets us more excited.
or
B. It helps us to be compassionate.

66. If you had a dial that could just turn down the level of activity of your sympathetic nervous system, this would be extremely useful in the art of staying cool. There's no such dial, but if you practice enough, you can learn to turn down your sympathetic nervous system activity at will! You do it by practicing one or more relaxation strategies.

The message is that

A. People once thought that we have no voluntary control over our sympathetic nervous system activity.
or
B. By practicing various relaxation techniques, you can learn to turn down your sympathetic nervous system activity.

67. Here's an example of one of those strategies. It's called "breathe and relax." You sit down in a place without stimulation (turn off all electronics) and close your eyes. You become aware of the rhythm of your breathing. You don't try to speed it up or slow it down; you just observe it. Then, each time you inhale, you get into mind a muscle or group of muscles in your body -- your face and head, your neck, your shoulders, your upper arms, your forearms, back, abdomen, upper legs, or lower legs. Each time you exhale, you try to make that muscle group more loose, limp, and relaxed than it was before. You want to practice at times other than when

something is exciting or distressing you, and get so competent at turning down your level of arousal that you can do it when you need to keep your temper.

What's a summary of the technique described in this text unit?

A. As you breathe in, get some muscles in mind; as you breathe out, try to make those muscles more relaxed.
or
B. Exercise your muscles so that some fatigue helps you in the process of relaxing them.

68. How often, and how long, should you practice muscle relaxation? Traditionally people have meditated or practiced relaxation for perhaps 10 to 20 minutes, twice a day. But people have reported really good results in reducing tension-related problems by using a schedule of relaxing the muscles for only a couple of seconds, around 50 times a day. The most frequent reason that relaxation techniques don't help is that they aren't used. So whatever schedule of relaxation you can actually follow is the one that is best!

The author feels that relaxation or meditation should be done

A. once in the morning, and once in the evening, for 10 minutes each,
or
B. for whatever length of time and a frequency works best for you?

69. Here's another relaxation technique, called the "good will meditation," or "loving kindness meditation. You sit down, relax your muscles briefly, and then wish these three things for yourself:

May I become the best I can become.
May I give and receive kindness.
May I live in compassion and peace.

And then, you picture someone else -- family member, friend, even enemy. You wish the same things for that person. Then you picture another person, and another, and wish those things for each person in turn.
What's a summary of what was just advised?

A. You sit silently and let your thoughts go, without trying to direct them, and observe what they do.
or
B. You sit silently and have good wishes for yourself and other people.

70. Here's a third meditation technique, called the kind acts meditation. You look at the following list of types of kind acts:

Helping
Teaching
Complimenting
Thanking
Being a good listener
Having a good conversation
Consoling

Giving good wishes
Giving a gift
Spending time with
Entertaining
Physical affection when and if
appropriate
Doing something fun with
Not spoiling

      For the kind acts meditation, you go down the list, and imagine any person doing a kind act of that sort, for anyone else. When you reach the end, you start back at the beginning. In subsequent trips through the list, you can imagine new kind acts or re-imagine old ones, whichever you want.

What's a summary of this text unit?

A. In the kind acts meditation, with the aid of a list of types of kind acts, you simply imagine anyone doing kind acts for anyone else.
or
B. The behaviors that we actively and repeatedly imagine tend to be acted out in real life.

71. The last kind act on the list, "not spoiling," refers to times when the kindest thing to do is not to give someone what he or she wants -- for example, not giving candy to a child who hopes to get it by having a tantrum; not lending money to a relative who will spend it on heroin, etc. This item reminds us that kindness doesn't consist in doing for everyone what that person happens to want. But it's possible to "not give" to another person in a kind and non-hostile way.

What's another way of expressing the point of this text unit?

A. A form of meditation is to think about caring for oneself and caring for others, and seeing what sorts of concrete images come to mind when one thinks about these ideas.
or
B. Kindness does not consist in just doing whatever someone wants you to do, but rather doing something that helps the person in the long term.

72. Why are images of kindness relaxing? Because the circumstances in which we have to flee or fight are when something unkind is about to happen. Acts of loving kindness are the opposite of what makes us tense, scared, or angry.

What's a summary of this text unit?

A. Images of kindness are relaxing because they are the opposite of the sort of threatenig situations that stimulate the flight or fight response.
or
B. One of the major ways of reducing anxiety and anger is by putting into perspective how awful, or not awful, the situation is.

73. For any relaxation or meditation technique, you'll find from time to time that your mind drifts away from what you're trying to do, and you think about what happened earlier, what you need to do for tomorrow, a television show you watched, or something else off track. When this happens, and you become aware of it, you don't get down on yourself, but gently turn your attention back to the meditative technique you are using.

What's a summary?

A. When you are meditating, consider it normal if your attention wanders; don't get down on yourself when this happens, but just gently bring your attention back.
or
B. It's good to contemplate the question of what is really worthwhile, what are the best ways to spend your time and energy.

74. An aid to relaxation practice is biofeedback. This consists in measuring something your body is doing, some physiological variable, and seeing if you can learn to control it voluntarily, usually via relaxation methods.

When you relax, you'll find that your heart rate goes down. Because your blood vessels in your hands and feet get a little wider, the temperature of your fingertips tends to go up. You can monitor these, just to get a read on how much you're turning down your sympathetic nervous system. For about $15 you can buy a "pulse oximeter" which when clipped onto your fingertip, gives you a continuous read of your heart rate. It's fun to see the heart rate go down as you relax. For about $25 you can buy a biofeedback thermometer that measures your fingertip temperature. Aas you relax you notice your hands getting warmer. Electronic measures of your muscle tension are quite a bit more expensive, but you don't really need them, if you can train yourself to recognize how tense your muscles are. You can directly sense how hard your muscles are pulling.

Lots of practice in relaxation will increase your ability to purposely calm yourself when you need to!

What's a summary?

A. Muscles can be working hard by tensing, even when they are not moving.
or
B. It's fun and useful to measure heart rate or fingertip temperature and see if you can learn to control them voluntarily with relaxation techniques.

Influencing your feelings by choosing thoughts

75. Imagine two employees; both of them get "chewed out" by their boss. While this is going on, the first is thinking, "What a _____(taboo word) that guy is! Who does he think he is, insulting me like this! I'd like to let him have it, right in the jaw!"

The second is thinking, "OK, this doesn't feel good, getting criticized, but I can handle it. My goal is to stay cool and listen carefully and learn as much as I can about how to do things better. If I can stay cool, I'll deserve to feel really good about how I handled this!" Which employee, do you think, finds it easier to stay calm? Which one is less likely to lose his or her temper? My bet is on the second one.

What's a summary?

A. The employee who thinks angrier thoughts gets angrier, and vice versa.
or
B. Criticism happens, so you'd better get used to it.

76. This illustrates a very important principle: what we say to ourselves, our self-talk, greatly influences our emotions and our behaviors. This is very important, because we can choose what we say to ourselves, especially if we practice the types of self-talk that we think will be most useful. These two sentences sum up the most important insights of cognitive therapy, which was one of the most helpful inventions of the twentieth century.

Which are the two ideas that the author says are the main concepts of cognitive therapy?

A. Monitor your weekly use of time, and schedule more of the activities you find useful or pleasant.
or
B. Your thoughts greatly influence your feelings and behavior; you can learn to control your thoughts.

The twelve thought system

77. When we pick our self-talk, it's very useful to have some labels for the different types we might pick. The following twelve classes of thoughts form a system that has proven very useful for lots of people. These categories seem to cover the possibilities remarkably well. I'll illustrate each of them with the situation we just mentioned, i.e. getting criticized by a boss.

What's the point of the 12 thought classification system?

A. To help you realize what sort of errors you are making in your thought processes.
or
B. To help you pick which sorts of thoughts you want to think in any given situation.

78. Here are the twelve types of thoughts:

1. Awfulizing. This is bad; I'm in trouble.
2. Getting down on myself. I screwed up, I blew it.

3. Blaming someone else. He's not being nice about this.

4. Not awfulizing. This isn't the end of the world; I can handle this.

5. Not getting down on myself. I don't want to waste my energy punishing myself for this.

6. Not blaming someone else. Going over and over how unpleasantly he's acting won't help me.

What type of thought is it when someone thinks, "Oh no! I can't stand this!"

A. Not getting down on himself or herself?

or

B. Awfulizing?

79. The list of the twelve thoughts continues.

7. Goal-setting. My goal is to stay cool and calm and listen and learn as much as possible.

8. Listing options and choosing. I can relax my muscles, I can reflect back what I'm hearing to make sure I understand it correctly. I can say that I'm sorry I made that mistake. I can say thanks for explaining this to me. I think I'll choose all four of those options.

9. Learning from the experience. I learned from this that in the future, I should do this differently:_____.

10. Celebrating luck: I'm lucky that this wasn't a worse mistake than it was.

11. Celebrating someone else's choice: I'm glad the boss decided to explain this to me instead of firing me.

12. Celebrating my own choice: I'm really proud of myself for keeping calm and listening well!

Someone thinks, "In handling this situation, my first priority is to come across as a reasonable person." This type of thought is

A. Listing options and choosing,

or

B. Goal setting?

80. There is no one of these twelve thoughts that you should avoid altogether. The big idea of the twelve thought classification is that you can choose which thoughts are most useful, rather than being stuck in the sort of self-talk you happen to be in the habit of.

Someone says to someone else: "You're awfulizing! You shouldn't do that!" Does the author endorse that sort of staement?

A. No, because sometimes it's very useful, or even essential for survival, to recognize how bad or dangerous a certain situation is.

or

B. Yes, because awfulizing tends to make people feel unpleasant feelings.

81. People do get themselves in trouble by overdoing the first three, and I do

recommend avoiding "overdone" versions of them. Here are some examples of "overdone" awfulizing, getting down on yourself, and blaming someone else for the same situation:

1. Awfulizing (overdone): I can't stand this! This is terrible, this is the worst thing that ever happened to me! Oh, no, no! What will become of me -- something terrible!
2. Getting down on myself (overdone): I can't do anything right. I screw up everything. I'm a worthless employee, and a worthless person altogether!
3. Blaming someone else (overdone): What a horrible person he is, saying these things to me! He deserves to be blown up!

This "overdone" self-talk tends to make the person feel more anxious, more guilty or demoralized, or more angry than is useful to feel.

What attitude toward unpleasant emotions such as fear, guilt, and anger does the author imply in this text unit?

A. They are useful when they provide signals or motivation to deal with unwanted situations; they can be harmful when they are overdone.
or
B. Anger can in certain circumstances be pleasant, when the person is unquestionably dominant over the person to whom the anger is directed?

The twelve thought exercise

82. The twelve thought exercise is meant to increase your mental flexibility, to increase your ability to pick any of the twelve thoughts that might be useful in the situation you're in. To do the exercise, you think of one situation -- any situation, wanted or unwanted -- and make up an example of each of the 12 thoughts having to do with that same situation. What we did previously, with the situation of being criticized by the boss, is an example. Let's give one more example. This time the situation is that someone at work says something and other people laugh, but I don't understand why it's funny. I'm not sure whether the person is teasing me or not.

What's the point of the 12 thought exercise we're about to illustrate?

A. To help you realize that there are lots of different ways of reacting to any given situation, and to practice generating the different types of thoughts.
or
B. To help you practice realizing what the definitions are of the types of thoughts.

83. Here goes the 12 thought exercise:

1. Awfulizing (without overdoing it): I don't like this. They seem to be in on something that I'm not.

2. Getting down on myself (without overdoing): This may be an example of the sort of social situation that I'm not very good at.

3. Blaming someone else (without overdoing): I wish the person had made what he said easier for me to understand.

4. Not awfulizing. I can handle this. If some things that people say go over my head, that's not the end of the world.

5. Not getting down on myself: It won't do any good to punish myself for the fact that this sort of thing isn't my greatest srength.

6. Not blaming someone else: People do these humorous things that I don't understand sometimes, and I can't expect them not to, just to accommodate to me.

7. Goal-setting. My goals are to stay calm, be polite, and be appropriate.

8. Listing options and choosing: I could ask the person to explain. I could try to remember what he said and just ponder it later. I could just let it go and figure it probably isn't too important. It feels fairly unimportant to me, so I'll let it go, and if it keeps coming back up, I'll politely ask the person to explain it to me.

9. Learning from the experience: I learned from this that I don't have to understand everything completely to get by and do an OK job of socializing.

10. Celebrating luck. I'm lucky that I can understand much more than I can't understand.

11. Celebrating someone else's choice: I'm glad the person is being lighthearted and relaxed rather than mean.

12. Celebrating my own choice: I feel good about myself for staying cool and not worrying too much about this.

What would have been an example of awfulizing with overgeneralization or overdoing it?

A. I don't like this situation; it makes me uncomfortable.
or
B. I just can't stand this! This is horrible not to know what's happening!

The four thought exercise

84. When you're in a real life situation, you usually don't have time to go through all the twelve thoughts right on the spot. However, you often do have time to go through a shorter version, where you do the following four:

not awfulizing
goal-setting
listing options and choosing
celebrating your own choice.

Why do the four-thought exercise rather than the complete twelve-thought exercise?

A. The other eight thoughts really aren't necessary.
or
B. The four thoughts can be done quickly enough to be a useful response to unwanted situations in real life.

85. Let's imagine the situation wherein I've been working at the computer, but my last 15 minutes of work gets irretrievably lost.

Here go the four thoughts:

Not awfulizing: Well, it's only 15 minutes. So that's not so bad.

Goal-setting: My main goal is to stay cool and calm, not to raise my voice, not to hit anything with the palm of my hand, and so forth. My second goal is to get back the work I lost and not to lose it again.

Listing options and choosing: I can take a little break, to cool off. I can relax my muscles for just a few seconds. I can start right back in to doing the work over again while it's still fresh in my mind. I'm choosing to relax my muscles for just a few seconds, then jump right in to typing the work over again before I forget it. Also, this time I'll back it up on two different media as I go along.

Celebrating my own choice: Hooray! I handled this situation like a champ!

Which of the four thoughts is actually meant to result in positive feelings, even though the situation was unwanted?

A. listing options and choocing, or
B. celebrating your own choice?

Repetitive fantasy rehearsal with provocations.

86. How do you become an expert at emotional regulation and anger control? Here's a program:

1. You develop a list of possible provocations: anything that has angered or upset you in your whole life, anything you can imagine happening that would anger or upset you, or even a list of provocations that someone else has made up.

2. You practice doing the 12 thought or the 4 thought exercise with those situations, not just once, but many times.

3. You try especially hard to think of reasonable, mature, wise options when you get around to listing options and choosing.

In doing this, you are taking advantage of the principle of fantasy rehearsal. The phrase *fantasy rehearsal* refers to the fact that practicing something in your imagination makes it easier to do in real life. Countless experiments have demonstrated this principle. It is one of the most important ideas for emotional regulation, because it's much easier to think of wise options in fantasy situations, when you have plenty of time and there is no pressure, than in real-life, especially at the beginning of your mission.

Which of the following is the better summary of this text unit?

A. To get good at anger control, practice twelve or four thought exercises with many imaginary provocations, trying hard to generate good options.
or
B. The ability to list many good options in response to hypothetical situations is an ability that is correlated with mental health.

Alternatives to hostile or violent behavior

87. Here are a few nonviolent, non-hostile options to consider in provocation situations.

Ignoring. Sometimes the best response to some unwanted behavior that someone else does is just to ignore it, to do nothing.

Differential reinforcement: This means ignoring the unwanted behavior and trying to respond positively when the person does something you like. Over time, this can sometimes influence the person to do more of what you like.

Assertion: This means calmly and politely asking the person to do what you want. "Could you please stand just a little farther away when you speak with me? It makes me feel more comfortable."

Conflict-resolution conversation: State the problem, listen carefully to the other person's ideas about the problem, list options together, think about the advantages and disadvantages of the options, try to agree on some option, and stay polite the whole time. There's more about this in another chapter.

Someone has a strategy of responding in a very low-key, non-excited way, or not responding at all, to any unfriendly comments of other people, and responding in a friendly and enthusiastic way to friendly comments of other people. This strategy is called

A. Differential reinforcement
or
B. Assertion.

88. Here are more strategies for responding to provocations:

Relaxation: Relax the muscles so as to help yourself keep calm.

Rule of law: Appeal to some authority or rule-maker, or to an actual law, to help with the decision.

Away from the situation: When anger is too great, try to politely move away from the other person.

Friendly behavior: Being pleasant and friendly, even when the other person is mad.

Tones of voice: Speak not too loudly, not too fast, not too high pitched.

The mnemonic Ida Craft may help you remember these options.

Someone is being harrassed by a coworker. The person first clearly asks the coworker to cease the behavior; when that doesn't work, the person goes to the supervisor to report this. The two strategies the person used were

A. Tones of voice, then ignoring.
or
B. Assertion, then rule of law.

Non-punitive sources of power

89. Sometimes people resist giving up the habit of losing their temper. Why? One reason is that getting mad can sometimes give you power over people -- the type of power that says, "If you want me to quit raging at you, you'd better do what I want you to do." But this type of power doesn't work well in the workplace. Fortunately, there are other ways to get the power to influence people to do what you'd like them to do. Let's look at some of them.

This text unit implies that one of the payoffs that sometimes reinforces anger is

A. the good feeling of letting anger out,
or
B. the fact that anger and aggression are ways of exerting power over other people.

90. Here are non-punitive, non-aggressive sources of power:

Reciprocity. This means that you do things to help out the other people, and as a result they are motivated to do things to help you out. Partly, they want to pay you back, and partly they want to keep your good behaviors coming.

Money. One great way to get someone else to do something is to pay them to do it. And sometimes just having money gives you power without your having to actually pay people. This is a great reason for being employed, not wasting money, and investing well.

Competence in valued skills. When you're the best in some valuable skill, or even when you're "good enough" at it, that competence leads people to do things you want in order to get your competent behaviors.

Work capacity. If you're capable of doing a lot of valuable work without needing to rest, your productivity creates value that other people are willing to do things for you in order to get.

Friendship. When people like you, they want to please you more.

Walk-away power. Suppose a boss is treating you badly. One of the most important sources of power you could have is the knowledge that you could get hired at two or three other places if you quit this job. If your boss knows you can "walk away," he or she is more motivated to do what is necessary to get you to stay, than if he or she is under the impression that you are "captive" to this one job.

Someone has great skill at statistical analysis. The person gets offers from other companies to work for them, and the person is mobile enough that the person could take one of those offers easily. When the person asks politely for a change in work location to a more private place, the supervisors accommodate the person quickly. Which of the above-mentioned sources of power is the person using?

A. friendship and money,
or
B. competence in valued skills and walk-away power?

91. Here are more non-punitive sources of power:

Assertion. Simply being able to ask for what you want, calmly and politely, conveys a certain amount of power to get it. A surprising number of people don't feel they can use this power.

Verbal persuasion. If you have the ability to point out, clearly and articulately, why one option is better than another, this increases your power to influence others.

Ethics. If you have a good sense of what is right and wrong, and you are advocating for what is good and right, this helps you to persuade.

Tolerance of others' hostility to you. If you can handle it when people disagree with you or even insult you, you have more power than if someone can make you back down just by talking mean to you.

Organizing groups. People gain power by finding allies and acting as a group rather than taking on power struggles alone.

The law. If there are laws or legal precedents that reinforce your case, this can be a strong source of power.

Clear goals. Power means the ability to achieve your goals. Knowing clearly what your goals are is usually a necessary step in achieving them.

People in someone's company are contemplating doing something that an employee regards as morally wrong. The person gives a very clear and cogent speech in a meeting, explaining the reasoning. The person changes people's minds.

Which of the above sources of nonpunitive power did the person use?

A. ethics and verbal persuasion,
or
B. work capacity and friendship?

*   *   *

92. If you contemplate these more mature, more highly developed sources of power, I think you'll conclude that having tantrums or being violent is almost always unnecessary. These maneuvers are often the last resort of people who haven't developed the alternative sources of power highly enough.

The attitude toward physically hurting people or yelling at them in anger, that is expressed in this text unit, is that

A. Violence and verbal abuse are often in imitation of behaviors people have seen in the media,
or
B. Violence and verbal abuse are often signs that the person lacks the skills to use the non-punitive sources of power listed above.

Chapter 5: Emotional Regulation, Part 2: Anxiety and Aversions

93. When people talk about "anxiety disorders," they refer to problems caused by too much fear, worry, fright, or panic. Heights, public speaking, being in social situations, failing, certain animals, getting blood drawn, taking tests, elevators, being abandoned, having a dread disease (when one doesn't), intruders in the night, driving, riding in airplanes, the disapproval of others, certain bad memories, certain intrusive images -- all these and more are common situations that can get too much fear attached to them.

What's a summary of this text unit?

A. Lots of situations can have too much fear associated with them. Such situation-fear connections constitute the anxiety disorders.
or
B. Some fears are quite useful: they lead us to avoid danger. These are wanted or realistic fears.

94. Sometimes people have bad feelings other than fear attached to certain situations -- feelings of disgust, shame, or just an unspecified bad feeling. Rather than speaking of these as fears, we can refer to them as aversions -- some aversive feeling is attached to the situation. Fears are a very important type of aversions. We reduce unwanted non-fear aversions in much the same way that we reduce unwanted fears.

What's a summary of the above text unit?

A. When situations have unpleasant emotion of any sort, not necessarily fear, attached to them, we call those associations aversions.
or
B. Relaxation techniques are helpful in reducing aversions.

Some aversions are good

95. Evolution came up with fears and aversions to help us stay alive. We're born with a fear of going over cliffs, and with good reason -- those without such a fear got selected out by evolution. It's good to fear traveling at dangerously high speeds in cars. It's good to fear poisonous snakes, getting into fights with powerfully dangerous people, doing things that destroy your reputation, eating contaminated food, and so forth. It's good to have aversions to noises so loud as to damage your hearing, poisonous plants, and others.

So here's the first question to ask about an aversion: Is it good for me, or not? Is it wanted, or unwanted, realistic, or unrealistic? If the answer is that it's good for you, wanted, and realistic, you don't try to reduce the fear; you just try to avoid the harmful situation. For example, I have a fear of riding in a car at 100 miles an hour along residential streets on snowy nights. I don't want to reduce that fear, but just to avoid that situation, for the rest of my life.

What's a summary of the above text unit?

A. What you say to yourself about a situation has a lot to do with how aversive it is.
or
B. Some aversions are realistic and useful; in those cases the goal is to avoid the harmful situation, not to reduce the fear or aversion.

96. For the rest of this chapter, let's think about how you reduce unwanted fears or aversions. We'll do this mainly by explaining certain terms used by anxiety-reduction specialists. If you understand each of these, you understand the general plan for reducing fears or aversions.

What's a summary?

A. From here on out we're talking about how to reduce unwanted fears and aversions.
or

B. Lots of repetitive practice is usually necessary in reducing unwanted fears.

SUD level

97. SUD is an acronym for "Subjective Units of Distress" (or Discomfort, or Disturbance). This is a rating of how much discomfort or suffering you are experiencing at any given time. Often the rating is on a 0 to 10 scale, with 0 meaning no bad feelings, and 10 meaning extremely unpleasant bad feelings. The bad feelings can be fear, disgust, feeling grossed out, feeling angry, or any other unpleasant feelings.

When there is fear or aversion attached to a situation, one of the important questions is, how unpleasant is it? You usually want to work with easier situations first, usually meaning the ones with low SUD levels attached to them (maybe 4 and under) rather than "jumping into the deep end" by trying to conquer the 8's, 9's and 10's on a scale of 10.

What's a summary?

A. The SUD level is a rating of how aversive a situation is, e.g. on a scale of 0 to 10. In reducing fears you start with the low SUD level ones rather than going straight to the scariest ones.
or
B. When you imagine scary situations vividly, you can measure the effects on

heart rate and other physiological variables.

Mastery versus avoidance choice point

98. This is the choice: "Do I want to get over this aversion (called mastery), or do I just want to stay away from the situation that I have an aversion to (called avoidance)? If the fear really gets in the way, we're usually in the situation where avoidance feels more comfortable at any given moment, but mastery makes us happier in the long run. These are the sorts of situations where self-discipline is called for.

What's a summary?

A. The fears you want to work on the most are those that subtract the most from your overall happiness rating.
or
B. The mastery versus avoidance choice point necessitates the decision whether to work to get over an aversion, or just to avoid the aversive situation.

Internal sales pitch

99. The internal sales pitch is a list of reasons why you want to go for mastery rather than avoidance. What are the payoffs that may come from achieving mastery, i.e. getting rid of the unrealistic fear? When you are wavering as to whether you really want to do the hard work of fear- or aversion-reduction, it's good to have memorized the reasons why you want to accomplish your goal.

Which of the following would be likely to be listed on an internal sales pitch for getting over a fear of social situations?

A. So that I can have more friends and be less lonely.
or
B. It's helpful for me not to breathe too fast when I'm in this situation.

Hierarchy

100. A hierarchy is a list of things arranged in some order from least to most. In the fear-reduction realm, the hierarchy is a list of situations in order of their SUD level. It's important to find some situations that have a small and moderate SUD level. If entering a social group where the agenda is standing around and talking produces 9 on a scale of 10 SUD level, what's the SUD level for just *imagining* yourself doing that? How about the SUD level for imagining *someone else* doing that? How about seeing someone else do that on a television screen that is far away from you? How about reading a dialogue of social conversation that someone else has written? These are the sorts of situations that people assess in order to get a

hierarchy that starts low and gradually goes up.

What does the word hierarchy mean, for the purposes of this book?

A. A list of tasks or challenges or situations listed in order of how difficult they are to handle.
or
B. A system for running an organization where bosses have bosses, who have other bosses, and so forth, so there is a system of ranks.

Habituation and desensitization

101. The words habituation and desensitization both refer to getting used to a situation, the longer you are exposed to it. As you get used to the situation that brings forth unrealistic fear or aversion, the SUD level falls. Habituation refers to the simple fact that the longer and the more times you are exposed to the same situation, with no negative consequence following, the less the situation tends to evoke bad feelings. The word desensitization usually refers to using exposure, hierarchy, and habituation, often with relaxation also, to reduce or eliminate a fear or aversion.

When habituation or desensitization takes place, what happens, by definition?

A. People speak to themselves in less excited tones of voice.

or
B. A situation elicits less emotion than it did before.

Exposure

102. To do an exposure is to put yourself in a situation that brings forth a fear or aversion, so you can habituate, or get used to, that situation. Another way of viewing exposure is that it gives you the opportunity to practice handling the situation well. Usually you start exposures with situations fairly low or moderate in SUD level rather than those at the top of the hierarchy.

Why do you think that nearly all successful anti-anxiety programs involve exposure?

A. Because to handle a situation less fearfully, you need to practice handling that situation.
or
B. It's good to be able to get allies to help you out when you need them, in getting over aversions.

Long-enough exposure

103. By "long enough," we mean long enough for habituation to take place. Long exposures tend to reduce SUD levels and eventually get rid of fears and aversions. Brief exposures followed by escape from the exposure situation, on the

other hand, tend to make fears and aversions stronger. Why? Because escaping is powerfully reinforced (or rewarded) by the relief from fear that you get. Thus the next time you are in the situation, you will tend to want to escape even more, because you were powerfully rewarded for escaping. And "wanting to escape even more" is about the same thing as "being more afraid!"

What's a summary?

A. Staying in a scary situation long enough to get used to it tends to reduce fears, whereas escaping as soon as the SUD level rises tends to make fears worse.
or
B. Thinking about the chances of something bad happening, and how bad that outcome is, helps in deciding how much actual danger you are facing.

Self-talk

104. Self-talk is what you say to yourself. If your self-talk during the exposure is "I hate this, I can't wait for this to be over, why am I doing this, I hate it that this is so hard for me," then habituation doesn't come as fast, or maybe not at all. If the self-talk is "Hooray, I'm doing something really courageous and self-disciplined; I'm accomplishing something really useful for myself," then habituation usually comes faster and easier.

We mentioned earlier that making exposures too brief can be a reason why fear reduction doesn't work. What other reason was mentioned in this text unit?

A. The presence of lots of negative self-talk that makes the situation continue to be aversive.
or
B. The fact that the person really believes, deep down, that the fear is realistic?

Fantasy rehearsal

105. Fantasy rehearsal means practicing something, like a deliberate exposure with habituation and useful self-talk, in your imagination rather than real life. It is extremely useful that we can practice in imagination as well as in real life.

What would be an example of fantasy rehearsal?

A. Someone with a fear of swimming dangles her feet in the shallow end of a pool.
or
B. Someone with a fear of swimming imagines herself walking around in the shallow end of a pool.

Coping rehearsal

106. A coping rehearsal is a fantasy rehearsal in which you imagine yourself

having a SUD level with an exposure, but using self-discipline so as to keep up the exposure long enough. Usually you imagine the SUD level going down over time.

In a coping fantasy rehearsal, you imagine that

A. the situation is easy for you,
or
B. the situation is difficult to handle, but you handle it well anyway?

Mastery rehearsal

107. A mastery rehearsal is a fantasy rehearsal in which you imagine that some miracle (or some hard work) has taken away all the bad feelings associated with the situation, and now you are able to handle the situation with comfort and pleasure and no distress at all.

Someone with a fear of social conversation imagines himself at a party, chatting with people pleasantly and having a good time, feeling totally comfortable. Is this a

A. coping rehearsal,
or
B. mastery rehearsal?

108. It's good to do coping rehearsals, because you are probably going to need to deal with a SUD level in your process of desensitizing yourself, so it's good to be prepared. It's good to do mastery rehearsals, because these are the way you eventually want to respond to the situation. So both of these are quite useful, and it's good to do them many, many times. You don't get very strong by lifting weights a few times and stopping. Similarly, you don't get rid of some fears by just doing a few fantasy rehearsals -- it often takes lots and lots of them.

What's a summary of this text unit?

A. To get over an unrealistic fear, do lots and lots of both coping and mastery fantasy rehearsals.
or
B. If you've had experience with getting physicall fit or stronger, this is helpful in getting over fears.

Fight or flight response

109. The fight or flight response is a reaction our bodies tend to have when responding to scary or aversive situations. We feel excited; our hearts beat faster; our hands sweat more; we tend to breathe faster; we secrete hormones like adrenaline; our blood pressures tend to go up; our muscles get tenser; our hands and feet get colder. The activity levels of our "sympathetic nervous systems" are turned up. (The sympathetic nervous system doesn't have much to do with sympathy.)

Riding on a ride at an amusement park that gives you the sensation that you are falling toward your death would tend to

A. Elicit the flight or fight response, and turn up the sympathetic nervous system activity,
or
B. Turn down the sympathetic nervous system activity?

Breathe and relax

110. As we discussed earlier in this book, breathe and relax is a relaxation/meditation technique; it is particularly tried and true for anxiety-reduction. You sit in a quiet place. You notice the rhythm of your breathing. Each time you breathe in, you notice any place in your body where your muscles are tense or tight, even a little bit. Each time you breathe out, you relax those muscles, even if only a little bit more than before. If you notice that your mind wanders from this activity, you don't get down on yourself for this, but simply bring your attention back to relaxing as you breathe. You don't try to breathe differently from what comes naturally. Turning down muscle tension tends to reduce anxiety, and to provide feedback to the brain that says, "Things are OK."

What's a summary?

A. Many meditation techniques involve some sort of attention to your breathing.
or
B. To use the breathe and relax technique, get a muscle group in mind as you inhale and relax those muscles as you exhale.

Mind-watching

111. Mind-watching is another method of relaxation/meditation. You sit quietly and relax. You let whatever comes into your mind come, and you simply observe what goes on, with a benevolent or kind attitude toward your own thoughts and feelings. You "save part of your mind to observe what the rest of it is doing." What goes on can include bodily sensations, things you hear or see, images that come to mind, thoughts that come to mind, or anything else you experience.

What's the mind watching technique of meditation?

A. You focus on something called a mantra, over and over, as you meditate.
or
B. You let your attention go to whatever comes naturally; you observe what your mind is doing with a benevolent attitude.

Kindness to self and others meditation

112. This is another method of relaxation/meditation. You sit quietly and relax. You wish that you will make and carry out the decisions that will increase the long-term happiness, health, and safety of yourself (this is kindness to self). You wish that you will make decisions that increase the long-term happiness, health, and safety of others (this is kindness to others). You spend time wishing these things about your own decisions. Then you wish the same thing for the decisions of another person, and another, and perhaps for humanity as a whole.

What might someone be saying to herself during the kindness to self and others meditation?

A. One... one... one ...
or
B. Caring for myself.... caring for someone else... being good to myself... being good to someone else...

113. Why practice these relaxation exercises? Because they help you get into a state where the flight or fight response is turned down, and to bring on that state at will. They help you practice being the opposite of distressed and anxious. Some daily practice of these techniques is a great thing for anyone who has had trouble with anxiety or aversions -- in other words, for almost all people.

Which group of people does the author think can benefit from relaxation/meditation techniques?

A. Those with anxiety disorders who have been diagnosed by a licensed professional.
or
B. Almost all people.

Four-thought exercise

114. As we discussed earlier: in the four-thought exercise, you think about a certain situation, using four different types of thoughts: not awfulizing (which is a conscious decision not to keep reminding yourself how bad the situation is); goal-setting (deciding what sort of outcome you're aiming for); listing options and choosing (figuring out several possibilities for what you want to do in this situation, and picking which one or ones you think are best); and celebrating your own choice (celebrating that you did the best you could in figuring out what to do).

The four thought exercise gives practice in rational thought, rational choice about what to do in the situation. This is another way of practicing an opposite of being overcome by anxiety or aversion.

Which are the four thoughts?

A. Not blaming someone else, good decisions, letting the mind wander, and concentration?

or

B. Not awfulizing, goal-setting, listing options and choosing, and celebrating your own choice?

Self-discipline

115. Self-discipline is the skill that lets you do something you don't feel like doing, or something that is relatively unpleasant, because you want to achieve a worthy goal. It takes self-discipline to do exposures and to do most of the other parts of the process of reducing fears or aversions.

Why does getting over fears and aversions take self-discipline?

A. Because if exposures are at the "just right" level on the hierarchy, they can be scary enough to be exciting in a fun way, but not scary enough to be unpleasant, like an exciting movie.

or

B. Usually, exposures in the short run are less pleasant than avoidance, even though they are more helpful in the long run?

PAST BAD and OH RAM PRISM

116. PAST BAD and OH RAM PRISM are mnemonics for ways of getting over unrealistic fears, as follows:

Probabilities and utilities: Figuring out the feared outcome, and then thinking, "How likely is that bad thing to occur?" and "How bad would it be?" If the bad thing isn't very bad, or if it's very unlikely, then you aren't in much danger, and reminding yourself of that tends to lower fear.

Allies: Getting a support system, not trying to do the mission all by yourself.

STEB and STEB revision: STEB stands for situation, thoughts, emotions, and behaviors. Figure out the situations that there are aversions to or fears of; be aware of what the habits are for thoughts, emotions, and behaviors in that situation. Then decide what thoughts, emotions, and behaviors you'd prefer for that situation, so you can practice them. Also practice the STEBS that constitute skillful, expert handling of the situation you are nervous about.

Tones of voice: Speaking to others or to yourself in calm tones of voice tends to make you feel calmer.

Someone with social anxiety thinks, "If I just act as nice as I can, the chance that anyone will think badly of me is fairly low, and even if that happens, it's not so terrible." Which method is the person using?

A. Allies,
or
B. Probabilities and utilities?

117. Now for more ways of fear-reduction.

Breathing: People often breathe too fast when they are anxious, and it's often helpful to slow down the breathing.

Activation versus relaxation: For most fears and aversions, it helps to become more relaxed. There are various methods of doing this.

Doing, not feeling as the sign of success: You don't worry too much about how you feel in the situation, but count it as a success if you can choose a good behavior and do it. This is especially true at the beginning of your fear-reduction efforts.

Someone feels the flight or fight response going off, but thinks, "My adrenaline is pumping, but I'm behaving reasonably in this situation. I'm succeeding!" That person is using the technique we named

A. activation versus relaxation.
or

B. doing, not feeling, as the sign of success?

* * *

118. The methods in the following list are more general methods for influeincing yourself or others to do anything, not just to reduce unwanted fear.

Objective-formation: Figuring out what your goals are and why you want to achieve them.

Hierarchy: Going along a gradual series of steps, starting with easier ones and working your way up.

Relationship: Having a good relationship with whoever is helping you -- including yourself!

Attribution: You *attribute* to yourself the potential to eventually succeed. Rather than saying "I can't do it," you might say, "I think the SUD level would be so high that I don't want to try it yet."

Modeling: You look at, or read about, positive ways of handling the situations.

A psychologist works with a child who is afraid of dogs by showing the child movies of other children gradually getting more comfortable with dogs. The method being used is called

A. Attribution.
or

B. Modeling.

119. Now for the final 5 of the general influence methods.

Practice: You rehearse the desirable patterns of thought, emotion, and behavior many times, in fantasy or in real life.

Reinforcement and punishment: You try to reward yourself and not to punish yourself for the desirable ways of doing things.

Instruction: You read or listen to directions on how to do it.

Stimulus control: Put yourself in the situations that bring out the desirable patterns.

Monitoring: Keep track of how you do over time; notice your improvement.

Someone wants to buy a certain book, and she also wants to get over a fear of being on bridges. She lets herself buy the book only after she has stayed on a bridge for 20 minutes. The method of influence she is using is

A. reinforcement,
or
B. instruction?

Summary: How to get over unrealistic fears and aversions

120. Here's a very condensed version of how to reduce unwanted fears and aversions. First, you make sure they really are unwanted. Then you make a list of reasons why you really want to go for mastery rather than avoidance (an internal sales pitch) and you memorize it. Then you create a hierarchy of situations, rating the initial SUD level of each. You start with situations low on the hierarchy, doing exposures that practice handling the situations well. You can practice using fantasy rehearsals, both coping and mastery, as a way of getting yourself ready for real-life exposures. You make sure the exposures are long enough and that your self-talk is self-reinforcing while you're doing the exposure. You work every day on relaxation techniques that help you turn down your flight or fight response at will. You practice not awfulizing, goal-setting, listing options and choosing, and celebrating your own choice in the scary or aversive situations. You keep practicing and gradually work your way up the hierarchy, and try to feel good about every positive movement you make. And that's it!

What's an even shorter summary of this summary?

A. List scary situations, rate their SUD level, work your way up the hierarchy,

use fantasy rehearsals to practice handling the situations, practice useful self talk, relax, use real-life exposure and practice if possible, and celebrate your successes.
or
B. Sometimes people think they can't get air when they in fact are breathing too fast and getting low on carbon dioxide. This can cause a vicious cycle. This can be interrupted by breathing more slowly.

121. If I had a dollar for every person who has been treated for anxiety with medication, but has never had any instruction whatever in the ideas of the above paragraph, I would have enough to start a very effective charitable foundation! This is true even though the ideas in the above paragraph have been validated by research findings "too numerous to count!"

The author regrets which situation in this text unit?

A. The situation where people waste money on luxuries rather than making sure that people have their necessities.
or
B. The situation where people get medication long-term for anxiety without having gotten any instruction in nonpharmacologic techniques.

Chapter 6: Celebrating Your Strengths

122. In this chapter we take a break from tackling some of the skills that folks on the autistic spectrum find difficult. A very important one of the twelve thoughts is "celebrating your own choice(s)." Recognizing and feeling good about the things you do well and the good choices you make will have two very important effects: 1) helping you do those good things more often, and 2) helping you to be happier!

In this text unit the idea is that

A. It's good not to brag to other people too much about the good things you do.
or
B. It's good to celebrate in your own mind and feel good about the good things you do, because those good feelings help you do more good things and be happier.

Are you able to tolerate tasks others find boring?

123. Some folks "on the spectrum" can tolerate repetition or technical details that others would find too aversive.

Are you able to stay on task without being tempted to socialize?

124. It is quite possible that if Isaac Newton had loved to go to parties and chat with friends, he would not have had time to invent calculus and first-year physics!

Someone asked Isaac Asimov how he was so prolific a writer. He replied that in order to be a prolific writer, two things are necessary: 1) you have to greatly enjoy writing, and 2) you have to not enjoy other things nearly as much. Having a "restricted range of interests" can sometimes be a strength.

An idea similar to those of this text unit is

A. There can be real advantages to finding things interesting that others don't find so interesting, especially if your interest can be useful.
or
B. Kind acts toward other people are a very important class of actions to celebrate.

Do you have a good memory for details?

125. Do you find yourself remembering street addresses, dates when things happened, passwords, model numbers of airplanes, train schedules, or such things without much or any effort? Learning computer programming in any language, or even learning to use any application, puts a large premium on remembering details. When do you use parentheses and when do you use curly braces? Some folks on the spectrum (definitely not all, and that's OK!) have gift for remembering such things easily; if you do, celebrate your acts of memory often!

Are you naturally honest?

126. According to employers, being honest is one of the most highly valued characteristics an employee can possess. Several folks I've known who are on the autistic spectrum seem to have been born with the habit of saying what they perceive to be true, and not bending the truth to try to make a better impression or achieve some secret goal. If you're like this, celebrate.

The two strengths mentioned in this text unit that are worth celebrating, if they are strengths of yours, are

A. empathy and social conversation skills,
or

B. memory for details and honesty?

Are you good at thinking outside the box in problem-solving?

127. The notion that energy and mass can be changed into one another, the notion that time slows down the faster you move, and other parts of Einstein's theories are quintessential examples of "thinking outside the box." You don't have to revolutionize physics to be good at coming up with creative ideas that others are too conventional to entertain. If you find yourself generating unconventional ideas that nevertheless prove to be useful, that's a reason to feel great about yourself.

The attitude toward unconventional ideas in this text unit is that

A. Escape from conventional thinking sometimes results in great advances.
or
B. When in Rome, you should do as the Romans do.

Can you hyper-focus?

128. Most of the folks on the autistic spectrum whom I've worked with have had difficulties with "transitions" -- meaning, they often greatly dislike it when someone says, "Stop doing what you're doing and do something else." My

guess is that Isaac Newton, who reportedly would become so focused on his work that he would forget to eat, would have responded with quite a bit of irritation if someone had ordered him to quit inventing calculus and work on social studies instead! The ability to focus for a long time on one task can lead to great productivity -- even though your work probably isn't as revolutionary as Newton's! If you find yourself able to lose yourself in a project, please celebrate that!

The skill mentioned in this text unit is

A. directing attention to something for a long time,
or
B. making people feel welcome?

Are you good at math, physics, chemistry, computers, engineering....

129. Many people on the autistic spectrum find themselves attracted to these topics, and talented at them. If you do, please celebrate. On the other hand, if you don't, that's OK! There are all sorts of different ways to be happy and successful.

The fields that were just mentioned

A. put a big premium on technical or mathematical skill,

or
B. put a big premium on "people skills."

The celebrations exercise

130. What have you done that you're glad you've done? This is a great question to ask yourself, often. There are two ways of doing the "celebrations exercise." One is to take turns with someone else telling each other specific answers to this question. A second is just to answer the question by yourself. A variation on the second is to keep a "celebrations diary," jotting down your own celebrations in a growing record that you can go back to repeatedly.

The celebrations exercise involves answering which question?

A. What am I grateful for?
or
B. What am I proud of doing?

Two broad categories of things to celebrate: the two big goals

131. Why do we want to be "mentally healthy?" What can we accomplish by mental health? I define mental health as the skills that enable us to achieve two big goals:

1. To promote our own long-term happiness.

2. To promote other people's long-term happiness.

There are several ways of expressing these two goals:

Caring for self and caring for others.
Meeting your own needs, and meeting others' needs.
Kindness to self, kindness to others.
Loving yourself, loving others.
"Love thy neighbor as thyself."
Enjoying life and helping others to enjoy their lives.
Making yourself better off; making others better off.

Any time you do anything that serves these two great goals, it's good to celebrate, just by thinking, "Hooray! I did something good!"

What's a summary of this text unit?

A. The two big pursuits this book advocates are being kind to oneself and being kind to others.
or
B. Some philosophers think that happiness is not achieved by focusing on achieving it, but as a by-product of other pursuits.

Categories of things to celebrate: The psychological skills list

132. How do you go about making yourself and others happier? Here's a list of a little more specific types of good stuff that you can do! The more you do these sorts of things, the more you tend to make yourself happy, and make others happy, not just for a moment, but for the long term.

1. Productivity

Getting work done, putting out effort.

2. Joyousness

Feeling good about your own accomplishments or kind acts, feeling grateful, feeling blessed, having fun, enjoying discovery, enjoying being with people, enjoying being alone…

3. Kindness

Helping, giving, teaching, complimenting, consoling, …

4. Honesty

Telling the truth, not deceiving, not cheating, not stealing.

5. Fortitude

Handling it well when you don't get what you want.

6a. Good individual decisions

Recognizing the choice points that are important; noticing the important aspects of those situations; getting clear on what outcome you want; getting information that helps with the decision; listing several options; predicting the advantages and disadvantages of the options; deciding; doing what you have decided; learning from the experience.

6b. Good joint decisions

Joint decisions are necessary in choice points where what is decided upon affects both people. They have to work together to come up with something that hopefully is good for both. It helps if they define the choice point without accusing or insulting or bossing the other person; if they each listen carefully to the other's views on the choice point; if they generate several options for what to do; if they don't criticize the options until they are finished brainstorming; if they discuss the advantages and disadvantages of the options rather than the good or bad points of the other person; if they finally agree on something; and if they are polite to one another throughout. The more you can influence the conversation in this direction, even if the other person makes

it difficult, the more you have to celebrate.

7. Nonviolence

If you totally avoid hitting, kicking, hurting, or killing, and totally avoid any threat or suggestion that you would consider such an action, you can celebrate your nonviolence! If you do anything to work toward a world where everyone avoids violent behaviors, you have even more to celebrate.

8. Respectful talk

Do you avoid insulting, name-calling, and tactless commands, contradictions, criticisms, and threats? Does what you say tend to make people feel good about themselves rather than hurt or angry or defensive? If so, celebrate your respectful talk!

Someone works in customer service and hears a lot of complaints from dissatisfied customers, some of whom are very rude. The person never even gets the urge to hit one of the customers, and is able to stay polite. This person is good at the skills of

A. Productivity and honesty,
or
B. nonviolence and respectful talk?

133. We continue with the 16 skills and principles.

70

9. Friendship-building

Any good chats with people? Good uses of greeting or parting rituals? Doing something fun with another person, spending some pleasant time with someone? If so, celebrate friendship-building!

10. Self-discipline

Were there times when you didn't feel like doing something, but did it anyway, so that you could achieve a goal? Or times when you felt very much like doing something, but avoided it, to help achieve a goal? These are self-discipline triumphs. For example: someone feels like playing a time-wasting but pleasant video game, but chooses to organize files and objects and papers instead.

11. Loyalty

Did you make any good decisions about whom you have commitments and obligations to, and whom you don't? Any times of sticking up for people who have been good to you? These are loyalty triumphs.

12. Conservation

Did you make a choice so as to avoid wasting money? Avoid wasting the earth's resources? Avoid wasting time? These are conservation triumphs.

13. Self-care

These are decisions that look after your own health and safety, or the health and safety of people you affect. Driving carefully, using seatbelts, eating healthy food, exercising, avoiding ear-damaging noises, avoiding addictive substances, avoiding sunburn -- all these are self-care triumphs.

14. Compliance

Are there times when you followed the rules or did what some authority (such as your boss) told you to do, even though you may not have felt like it? These are compliance triumphs.

15. Positive fantasy rehearsal

Any times of practicing in your imagination the good patterns you want to do more often? Any choices to avoid rehearsing violent or otherwise undesirable stories (for example by avoiding "shooter" games)? These are positive fantasy rehearsal triumphs.

16. Courage

Any times when you had a fear of something, or an aversion to something that wasn't really harmful or dangerous, and went ahead and faced that something anyway? These are courage skill triumphs, and these are the building blocks of getting over unwanted fears or aversions.

*   *   *

If you can play a game in your mind, each day, of seeing how many celebrations, how many positive examples, you can score, and also seeing if you can feel good about each one of them, this game will serve you well throughout your life!

Someone finds it fairly difficult to make new friends, but the person is very attentive and kind to the friends he already has, and never forgets them. The person has fewer celebrations in _____, and more of them in _____.

A. friendship-building; loyalty
or
B. honesty; courage.

Chapter 7: Social Conversation

The rhythm of social conversation

134. Here's what goes on in social conversation: People usually start out with greeting rituals. Then one person tells something about his or her own experience. This person stops talking often. The other person uses various responses to signal his or her interest in the topic, his or her understanding of what the speaker is saying, and the fact that he or she is listening and taking it in. These responses also reinforce, or reward, the speaker for telling about his or her experience. We speak of these responses as "listening" responses, although they are in fact spoken utterances.

When two people converse, they are not just taking turns giving information. This text unit includes something else important that they do, which is:

A. to log away in memory the information the other person is giving.
or
B. to send signals indicating that they are interested in, and understand, what the other person is saying.

135. In most conversations, the roles switch often. The listener becomes the talker, and tells about his or her own experience, and the talker becomes the listener, responding to what the other person is saying.

If the two people can

find topics they both enjoy talking and hearing about
reinforce or reward each other for talking
switch roles between talker and listener in a way that is pleasant for both

then social conversation can be a real art form, very pleasant for both people to participate in. If you can get very skilled at this art, you can increase your enjoyment of life, in addition to your success in the workplace! This art comes in handy almost every time people are with each other!

The author implies in this text unit that

A. Skill in social conversation is a large contributor to people's happiness, because it helps them enjoy being with other people.
or
B. While some people pick up social conversation skills just from observing it, others can pick it up best by studying the concepts and practicing using them.

The one minute rule

136. The "rhythm" of social conversation we referred to above has to do with turn-taking -- it's my turn to talk, now it's your turn, now it's mine again, and so forth. One of the most frequent ways that conversations turn unpleasant in which one person keeps talking too long. How long is too long? As a general rule, one minute is about the longest you should talk without giving the other person a chance to respond. Maybe the other person will say something that means, "I see, this is very interesting, please go on." In that case, you've been given another minute! On the other hand, if the other person changes the subject, doesn't respond at all, makes a summary of what you said in a way to conclude the topic, or does something else that doesn't cue you to keep going, it's time for you to cease and desist from what you were saying, and celebrate that you stopped to assess your listener's interest!

The one minute rule is that in social conversation, you should talk for how long without getting a clear signal from the other person that you should go on?

A. One minute or less.
or
B. At least one minute.

137. If you want to test the one minute rule, you might get a stopwatch and turn on a television news program where conversation is the agenda. One morning

I timed 19 utterances of invited guests in response to hosts' interview questions. The minimum was 16 seconds; the maximum was 77 seconds; the median was 35 seconds; the average (or mean) was 40 seconds. 84% of the utterances were under one minute. When the length of utterance approached 60 seconds, the probability that speaker would be interrupted appeared to become quite high.

Another readily available measure of how long it takes until people feel that "Your time is up!" can come from looking at advertisements on television. On a morning news program, there appeared to be three common durations: 15 seconds, 30 seconds, and 60 seconds. 35% of the ads were 15 seconds, 53% were 30 seconds, and 12% were 60 seconds. This is consistent with a report on the Internet that the majority of television commercials are 30 seconds long.

The information in this text unit suggests that the "one minute rule" may be

A. too short,
or
B. too long?

138. To give you one more perspective on how long people talk without stopping: for conversations portrayed in drama, such as movies and plays, the average length of utterance appears to be a great deal shorter than in interviews about current events. In Shakespeare's plays, for

example, Open Source Shakespeare reports that the average number of words per utterance ranges from about 18 words (in Two Gentlemen of Verona) to about 35 words (in Richard II). At a speaking speed of 125 words per minute, that translates into somewhere between 9 seconds and 17 seconds per utterance!

Apart from conversations, even the speeches in Shakespeare's plays are much shorter than many people's utterances. The "To Be Or Not To Be" soliloquy in Hamlet (including a brief utterance toward another character at the end) is 276 words and can be spoken in about 2.2 minutes. The "Friends, Romans, Countrymen" speech in Julius Caesar is divided into parts, the longest of which is also a little over 2 minutes.

The general idea of this text unit, as well as the previous two, is that

A. People are very interested in continuing to listen for a long time to useful or good information.
or
B. People get impatient and bored and irritated when someone speaks for too long without stopping, especially if the conversation is meant to be a typical social conversation based on turn-taking.

Four ways of listening

139. Most people find it more difficult to be good listeners than good talkers. If you can select well when to be silent, and when to use each of the following responses, you will usually come across as an excellent listener! Many shy people fear not being able to come up with something to say when it is their turn to talk. When in doubt, responding in one of the following four ways to what the other person just said is almost always appropriate. And these ways of listening often are good predecessors to telling about your own experience -- you seek first to understand the other person before asking the other to understand you.

Reflections
Facilitations
Follow-up Questions
Positive Feedback

The four ways of listening that we have just listed are ways that you

A. Enlighten the other person about something you know about,
or
B. React to what the other person said in a way that reinforces, communicates understanding of, or requests more of, what the other person has told you?

Facilitations

140. Facilitations are utterances like these:

Uh huh
Yes
I see
Humh

75

Oh. (or: Oh?)
Is that right.
OK
Yeah
What do you know?
I understand.
All right.
Wow
Humh!

These utterances all mean: "I'm listening, I'm tuned in; keep going if you'd like to." If they are spoken in a tone of voice of approval and enthusiasm, they also mean, "I'm glad you're telling me what you're telling me." These are extremely important messages. Eye contact and nodding the head "Yes" go along with these. Using facilitations, versus not using them, can make lots of difference in whether the other person feels positively reinforced, or rewarded, for talking with you.

The first person says, "I just got through running 10 miles!" Which of the following is a facilitation?

A. Sounds like you feel good about that accomplishment, right?
or
B. Wow!

Positive feedback

141. These are utterances that explicitly reinforce the other person's talking to you.

I'm glad you told me this.
Thanks for going into this with me.
Sounds like a good idea you have.
That's very interesting.
That's cool.
You have had some interesting insights.
Thanks for sharing that with me.

Someone says, "I had to work overtime until 2 a.m. last night." Which of the following is positive feedback?

A. Oh my. I'll bet you're exhausted today, huh?
or
B. Thanks for contributing to the cause in that way!

Follow up questions

142. These utterances ask the speaker to tell more about what the speaker is already talking about. If follow up questions are done well, they prompt the speaker to tell the next logical thing in the narrative or make the next logical point. They help the speaker communicated what the speaker wanted to communicate in the first place. When follow-up questions are done poorly, they ask about some irrelevant detail; having to respond is annoying to the speaker.

Here's a good follow-up question:

First person: I was driving here this morning, and there were these two guys, who came out right in front of my car and stood there, even after the light changed for me to go.

Second person: Strange! Do you think they were trying to block you, or were they just clueless about what was going on?

Here's a poor follow-up question:

First person: I was driving here this morning, and there were these two guys, who came out right in front of my car and stood there, even after the light changed for me to go.

Second person: Oh, what kind of car do you have?

The bad follow-up question was bad because it

A. insulted the speaker,
or
B. directed the speaker to go into something that didn't have to do with what she had started talking about?

143. Here's another pair of examples:

First person: This software is really well developed, and used mainly with command lines. Our assignment is to create a menu-driven interface for it.

Second person: I see. Please tell me more.

The open-ended follow-up question, "Please tell me more," invites the first person to keep going about any additional information he or she thinks relevant. It's a great all-purpose follow-up question. (By the way, grammatically, "Please tell me more" isn't a question, and doesn't end in a question mark. But it's a request for information, and has the same purpose as a question, so I count it as such.)

Here's a second example:

First person: This software is really well developed, and used mainly with command lines. Our assignment is to create a menu-driven interface for it.

Second person: Why would anyone want that, rather than just using the command interface?

The follow-up question is not as good as the first one. It may be irritating to the first person that the second person appears to be arguing with the assignment.

Let's give one more example of skillful and not-so-skillful follow-up questions.

First person: I'm looking forward to this week end. I'm headed for a festival.

Second person: Why are you doing that?

That wasn't a good follow-up question. Compare it with this:

First person: I'm looking forward to this week end. I'm headed for a festival.

Second person: Oh? What sort of festival?

Someone says, "I think our boss is irritated with me." Which is the better follow-up question?

A. Do you like that car that she drives? or
B. Oh? What makes you think so?

Reflections

144. A reflection is an utterance in which you paraphrase back to the person what you understood him or her to be communicating. You do this to make sure you understood right, and to let the other person know you understood. If you start a sentence in one of the following ways, and fill in the blank with what the other person communicated, you're doing a reflection.

So you're saying _____?
What I hear you saying is

_____.
In other words, _____?
So if I understand you right,
_____?
It sounds like _____.
Are you saying that _____?
You're saying that _____?

Someone says, "My hours have been getting cut back, a little more at a time." Which of the following is a reflection?

A. And if I understand you right, that's not a welcome change for you, correct? or
B. How much have they been cut back?

145. If someone does "good" or "skillful" reflections with you, it usually feels good -- you feel listened to, understood well; you feel that what you say is making an impact.. If someone does "bad" or "unskillful" reflections with you, it feels a little weird. For example:

First person: I don't know when I'm going to get all this stuff done! We're committed to have this accounting project done by the end of the week, and lots of people are counting on it. But I just don't see how it's going to be possible to finish anywhere close to then! Things are getting really tense!

Second person: It sounds like the time pressure is getting really oppressive. Sounds really unpleasant!

If I were the first person, I would feel as though I had been really understood. I would call the second person's response a "good" or "skillful" reflection. Now let's look at a different response to the same first statement.

First person: I don't know when I'm going to get all this stuff done! We're committed to have this accounting project done by the end of the week, and lots of people are counting on it. But I just don't see how it's going to be possible to finish anywhere close to then! Things are getting really tense!

Second person: You're saying that you're working on a project that's due Friday.

Why is this a "bad" or "unskillful" reflection? Because it misses the main point that the first person is trying to communicate. It's not inaccurate, but it overlooks the main thing the first person has feelings about, the main purpose that the first person had in speaking.

The author, in this last example, implies that a good reflection should

A. Respond to the main point the speaker is trying to make rather than a side issue.
or
B. Be succinct rather than excessively wordy.

146. Let's look at another example.

First person: There are some things I'm not sure about on this job. But my supervisor seems to act irritated when you ask questions about how you're supposed to do things. I feel pretty conflicted.

Second person: So you're saying you don't know how to do your job right.

This is a bad reflection -- why? It misses the point about the person's boss's reactions to questions. And worse, it paraphrases what the person said into a somewhat insulting statement. Let's redo the reflection, and turn it into a more skillful one.

First person: There are some things I'm not sure about on this job. But my supervisor seems to act irritated when you ask questions about how you're supposed to do things. I feel pretty conflicted.

Second person: So if I understand you right, your boss's reactions make you really hesitate to ask for guidance on how things should be done, and that's a pretty uncomfortable situation to be in.

This is a much better reflection. It paraphrases the main dilemma the first person is talking about.

Suppose the second person had instead said, "Sounds like you're feeling in conflict about whether to ask for guidance from your boss or not, right?" Do you think this is a

A. good reflection,
or
B. bad reflection?

147. Let's look at a third example.

First person: I love having an electric car! I never have liked gas stations, and especially now with global climate change, it's great not to be burning fossil fuel!

Second person: So if I understand you right, you don't like being in gas stations?

This isn't a good reflection -- it's missing the main point that the person is making. Let's try again.

First person: I love having an electric car! I never have liked gas stations, and especially now with global climate change, it's great not to be burning fossil fuel!

Second person: So if I understand you right, you get a real kick out of having a car that doesn't put carbon dioxide into the air and add to the climate change problem!

That's a much better reflection.
Suppose the second person had said, "If I understand you right, you have a phobia of gas stations?" Would this have been a

A. good reflection,
or
B. bad reflection?

148. It's possible to use reflections in a way that are really editorializing about your own opinions or arguing with the speaker. Don't use them this way. Here's an example:

First person: I love having an electric car! I never have liked gas stations, and especially now with global climate change, it's great not to be burning fossil fuel!

Second person: So you're saying it feels good not to be using gasoline, even if the power plant that creates the electricity burns oil or coal to make the electricity?

If you want to argue, don't enclose the argument in a reflection. Let the reflections be "pure" in their attempt to understand accurately, and communicate that understanding.

Suppose the first person says, "I ended up voting for Brown in the election."
The second person says, "So if I understand you right, you like candidates who care more about corporate interests than about the environment, huh?" Is the second person

A. editorializing through a reflection,
or
B. doing a "pure" reflection?

Putting telling and listening together: an example of social conversation

149. Now let's look at a little conversation, and label each of the moves that the people make in it.

Pat: Hi Lee! How's it going? (Greeting ritual.)

Lee: Hey Pat! Going fine, good to see you! (Greeting ritual.)

Pat: Hey, did you see that they opened up a little exercise room for us? (Telling about one's own experience or knowledge.)

Lee: No. That's interesting. (positive feedback) Please tell me more! (follow-up question)

Pat: I think the idea is that we sit around so much while doing our jobs, that it's not good for our health. So the idea of this is that we get up every now and then and just take a quick spin on a treadmill or exercise bike, or lift a few dumbbells, to have a break from the sitting. (telling about one's own experience or knowledge.)

Lee: Wow, thanks for letting me know about this. (positive feedback). Are you much of an exerciser, Pat? (follow-up question)

Pat: I'd say moderate. I never have been into competitive sports. I think that's partly because I never was much good at them. But I do like to go out walking. I'd like to go out biking if it weren't so darn dangerous. (telling about one's own experience)

Lee: I know what you mean about biking. Too much danger of being hit by a car, especially around here when they go so fast, right? (reflection)

Pat: Exactly. But there are some great walking trails around here, I'm discovering. There's an Internet site that tells where they are and how to get to them. (Telling about one's own experience.)

Lee: So technology makes it easier to know about how to get out into nature, huh? (reflection)

So far in this conversation, the person who has been in the "listener" role has been

A. Pat
or
B. Lee?

150. The conversation continues.

Pat: It sure does! How about you, Lee, are you into exercising? (follow-up question, signaling a shift from the talker role to the listener role.)

Lee: I'm like you, Pat; I'm not much into competitive sports. But I'm really glad to hear what you told me about the management encouraging taking exercise breaks, because I've been into high-intensity-interval work.

Pat: Oh? (facilitation) Tell me more, please. (follow-up question)

Lee: I've been reading on the Internet about how short bursts of really strenuous exercise -- like 30 seconds, as hard as you can go, maybe 10 or 20 times a day -- do really good things for your fitness level. Apparently it's possible to get into really good shape that way, with very little expenditure of time. (telling about one's own experience or knowledge.)

Pat: Interesting! (positive feedback) Is the idea that going all out stresses your body to get more fit, whereas the easier stuff doesn't stimulate improvement so much? (follow-up question)

Lee: That's right. But the other benefit for me is that I find that half a minute of maximal exertion helps me feel more alert and awake for a good while after that. (telling about one's own experience or knowledge.)

Pat: So if I understand you right, you've already been doing this, for breaks in your job, here? (reflection)

Lee: Yes. I'll have to say I've been a little sneaky about it. I have taken a quick trip outside, and a half a minute sprint down the sidewalk, followed by a walk back. Or sometimes a run up the stairs and a walk back down. (telling about one's own experience)

Pat: Is that right! (facilitation) Well I think you've already been doing just what they were trying to encourage us to do when they decided to put the little exercise room in! (positive feedback) But you've been trying not to attract attention when you do it, huh. (reflection)

Lee: I get the feeling that people still think you're weird if you just do a bit of exercise in some random place, don't you? Like, you don't see people doing jumping jacks or push-ups while they're waiting in line, and you don't see them hop up from their desks and do some squats, or that sort of thing. Even though it makes a lot of sense, it just isn't the custom, right? (telling about one's own experience)

Pat: I guess you're right. (positive feedback) And that's probably good, for the people who own gyms, but probably not so good for the fitness of people in general. (telling about own's own experience or ideas, returning to the speaker role)

Lee: Maybe some time we can go together down to the new little exercise place, and you can show me where it is. (an invitation)

Pat: I'd love to do that! I have some things to do now, but maybe later today I'll stop by and we can check it out. (responding positively to the invitation)

Lee: Sounds good. See you later! (parting ritual)

Pat: Yep, see you then! (parting ritual)

Is the author trying to give the impression that this conversation, for these imaginary people, was

A. pleasant,
or
B. unpleasant?

Listening to criticism, especially from a supervisor

151. Reflections, facilitations, follow-up questions, and even positive feedback are very useful to use when listening to criticism, especially from a supervisor. Being criticized is a very difficult situation for most people. Some people react to criticism with defensiveness or counterattack that actually makes things much worse for them. Let's look at an example where someone uses the same four listening techniques while being criticized.

Supervisor: Madison, could I talk with you a little bit in my office, please?

Madison: Sure.

Supervisor: There's a habit of yours that I'd be interested in your trying to change, please.

Madison: Oh? (facilitation) Tell me more about it, please. (follow-up question)

Supervisor: There are times when there's a meeting or a conversation, and someone will make a suggestion, and you will laugh pretty loudly at it. I think that habit detracts from the climate of the conversations.

Madison: OK.(facilitation) So you're saying that when I laugh when people say things, that hurts their feelings, huh? (reflection) Is it maybe that I'm giving them the impression that I think their answer is silly? (follow up question)

Supervisor: That's right.

Madison: I'm glad you told me about that, because I don't want to annoy people or be hurtful. (positive feedback) Can you remember any specific examples, just to help me remember them? (follow-up question)

Supervisor: Yes, when we were talking about the production techniques this morning, and Yannie was speaking about the loop.

Madison: OK, that's a helpful example. (positive feedback) You know, sometimes I laugh when I hear a good idea, one that I like, just like a little kid laughing for joy. But at other times I do laugh at ideas that I think are silly. I can see how people would not be able to tell the difference. (telling about one's own experience)

Supervisor: I see. (facilitation) So sometimes your laughter should really be taken as a compliment, if only there would be a clearer signal of that, huh? (reflection)

Madison: That's right. Well, thanks very much for calling this to my attention. (positive feedback) I'll see what I can do to improve things in this regard. (planning to ponder or problem-solve) Please let me know if it gets better or stays the same.

Supervisor: I'll do that. Thanks for listening. (positive feedback) I'll talk with you later! (parting ritual)

Madison: Yes, we'll be in touch! (parting ritual)

Do you think the author is depicting Madison as doing

A. an average, fair job of responding to criticism,
or
B. an uncommonly good job of responding to criticism?

Chapter 8: Using Organization Skills

152. Organizing means making plans, and carrying out those plans. It means figuring out how you are going to do something, and then doing it. It means creating a system for doing something, and then using that system. One major point of these plans and systems is to minimize the need to store information in memory. For example, if your papers are strewn all over everywhere at random, and you want to find one of them, perhaps you can do so, if you happen to remember where you put it. But if you have an organized filing system, you don't need to remember where you put every single piece of paper -- you look up the file for the category under which that paper falls; this is easy because the file categories are arranged alphabetically.

What's a summary of this text unit?

A. Organization skills keep you from having to remember so many things.
or
B. Organization skills lead other people to be impressed with your neatness.

What should be organized?

153. Here's a list of things to organize:

1. Time and tasks. What are the goals? How can they be accomplished? What to do, when to do it. Remembering what needs to be done. Making plans about what to do at what time, and executing those plans.

2. Stuff. Where do you put your physical objects?

3. Papers. How do you process and file them?

4. Electronic messages.

5. Computer files. Where they are stored, how they are named.

6. Ideas. When you speak and write, how do you organize the ideas you present?

Let's discuss each of these in turn.

Which did the author NOT include as one of the things to be discussed as something to organize?

A. What you have to do, and at what times, and for how long?
or
B. Your income and your expenses, i.e. your budget?

Time and Tasks

154. The most important aspect of organizing is figuring out what your goals are. If you know what you're trying to accomplish, it's much easier to accomplish it! In the workplace, what is the whole organization trying to do? What are the goals for your subunit, and what are you to accomplish? You might also write down your goals for work competence -- what do you want to get better at doing? Finally, you can write down your non-work goals: what are your goals for personal development, social relations, self-care, and so forth.

Often, in the workplace, your most pressing goal at any given time is to complete successfully a mission that has been assigned to you by your supervisor. When you get assignments, make sure you listen carefully. Use follow-up questions and reflections to make sure you understand. Make sure you know what a successful completion of this task would look like, how success is measured. If there is a deadline, make sure you know what it is. If there are several things that people want you to do, make sure you clarify the order of priority. Which is the most important task to complete next? If there are several tasks, it's good to write them down, and to number them in order of priority.

What's a summary of this text unit?

A. It's very important to know clearly what your goals are, what you are trying to accomplish. Sometimes it's very useful to write those down.
or
B. You want to avoid the situation where several different people are expecting different tasks to be done by you.

155. For any given task, what are the steps to carry it out? It's often really useful to write down these steps. This is a detailed plan about how you are going to accomplish the task. What are you going to do first, second, and so forth? What can you do alone, and what do you need to get others to help out on? Are there obstacles to completing the task successfully?

For many jobs, your duties are the same every day. For others, the important tasks change often. For the second type, a major organizing tactic is the daily to do list. These are the concrete, specific tasks that you want to accomplish today. It's good to number these in order of priority. What is the single most important thing to do today? This gets priority score 1. What's the second most important? This gets numbered 2. And so forth. When you get going, you work on the tasks in their order of priority. Each time you complete a task, celebrate in your mind. It's time to say, "Hooray, I completed a task! I did some productivity!"

Which of the following people do you think would need a written to do list and priority rating more?

A. A wait-person at a restaurant,
or
B. A plumber who gets calls from several customers and goes to their houses to do repairs?

156. Separate from the daily to do list, but often good to look at along with it, is the daily appointment calendar. This is where you write the things that have to be done by or at a certain time, for example meetings that occur at a certain time. The more frequently you look at your appointment calendar, the less likely you are to miss appointments and deadlines!

I'll leave it up to you to decide where and how to write and record these things. My preference is to write a goals list on a computer file, and a "master to do list" of things to be accomplished in the next few weeks in another computer file. I like to write the daily to dos and the appointments in a paper notebook, one for each month; for each pair of facing pages, one page is for daily to dos, and one page is for the appointment calendar. Many people are using their smartphones for appointments and daily to dos.

Which worker do you think needs an appointment calendar more?

A. a psychotherapist,
or
B. a writer of novels?

157. Suppose you have a project to complete by a date three weeks from now.

You would want to enter the deadline in your appointment calendar for that date. But also: figure out the subtasks, and create your own deadlines, and enter these in your appointment calendar too. You don't want to open your appointment calendar and find that something is due today that you should have been working on for three weeks!

When there are deadlines, set your own deadline earlier. For example, if the project is officially due in three weeks, your own internal deadline might be in two weeks and four days. Why plan to finish ahead of time? 1) You could get sick on the last day. 2) You could have a technological glitch. 3) You could realize you've underestimated the time the project takes. 4) You'll be less likely to have to stay up late at night. 5) You teach yourself to perform well when NOT under big time pressure.

What does the author's attitude seem to be toward people who feel that they perform best just before the deadline, and wait until the last minute to get started?

A. That these people probably get more work done than others.
or
B. That these people probably miss a lot more deadlines than others.

158. It's important not to overcommit. It's better to succeed at fewer things than to get burned out, or fail, trying to succeed at too many things at once. Every once in

a while, guess how long something will take to do, and then time how long it actually takes. Doing this helps you to make better estimates and plans. When someone asks you, "How long do you think it will take you to do X," you'll be better able to answer. You're less likely to fall into the trap where you promise more than you can deliver.

Which proverb summarizes this text unit?

A. A rolling stone gathers no moss.
or
B. Don't bite off more than you can chew.

159. Make use of routines. If you go to the same place at the same time each day and focus fully on work while there, you increase your chances of high productivity. You want to have your workplace become a "conditioned stimulus" that brings out efficient work.

    If concentration is a challenge for you, make things easier by eliminating distractions. Turn off your phone. Eliminate pop-up messages on the computer screen. Don't try to send and receive text messages.

    Here's a self-monitoring exercise for productivity. It's called the "concentrate, rate, and concentrate" activity. You work on a task for x length of time. You stop to rate how well you concentrated during that time -- how efficient and productive you were. You think about what contributed to or detracted from your productivity. Then

you work some more, and you rate yourself on the second round. Did you improve your productivity in round 2? And so forth. You alternate between working and monitoring how well you worked. And you also celebrate greatly when you have worked well!

What three methods of increasing productivity are recommended in this text unit?

A. Getting into routines, eliminating distractions, and monitoring your concentration.
or
B. Getting enough sleep, taking exercise breaks, and aiming for a speed of work that is in the "sweet spot" between too slow and too fast?

Organizing stuff

160. How do you avoid losing important things -- like your appointment calendar, phone, keys, wallet, identification card, flash drives, glasses, and so forth? You decide upon a "home" where that object is kept when it is not in use, and maybe a second home where it is kept in readiness for use. And you don't put the object down anywhere else! For example: my car keys are kept in one box on my desk, when I'm sleeping at night. Every morning, they go into my right front pants pocket. Those are the only two places where they are ever allowed to be, other than in my hand while unlocking a

door! Here is one custom that I think it pays to be quite rigid on.

How do you not lose your wallet, according to this text unit?

A. Severely limit the places you allow yourself to put it.

or

B. Fit it with an electronic unit that allows you to locate it using your cell phone?

161. Here's a second principle about objects: Don't let the homes for objects get too crowded and cluttered. Don't acquire too much stuff in the first place. The less you have, the easier it will be to keep up with what you do have.

What's a consequence of the idea in this text unit?

A. You can use acquiring a new object as a reward for doing something that requires self-discipline.

or

B. There comes a time where, when you get a new object, you need on the average to get rid of an old object to make room for it.

Organizing papers

162. Although they're being replaced by electronic messages, papers are still very important in signaling important items for the to do list.

First piece of advice on papers: don't let them accumulate too long without processing them. Some of them almost always will contain messages that "You need to do X by Y time or face Z consequence."

When you process them, think of these categories of action: 1. Toss. Into the recycling bin goes almost all the junk mail. 2. Refer to someone else. Sometimes (not too often) a paper needs to be handled by someone else and all you need to do is to give it to that person. 3. Action, immediate. The paper signals you to do something, and you do it, right away. 4. Action, deferred. You get your to do list, and put on it whatever the paper is signaling you to do. You put the paper in a file labeled "to do." Then when you get around to that task on your to do list, you pull out the paper, do what you need to do, and then either toss or file the paper. 5. File. These are the papers you don't need to do anything on now, but you need to keep for the future.

What's a mnemonic for the different things you can do with papers?

A. LISP,

or

B. TRAF?

163. When you are filing, ask yourself, "What category would I look under if I were searching for this piece of paper?" If there's already a file folder with that title, you put the paper in that file, at the end of

the stack. If there isn't, you pull out a new file folder and make one, stick the paper in it, and stick the folder in its place, alphabetically.

Organizing electronic messages

164. Emails and text messages can be just as overwhelming as papers, and they need to be processed frequently. It's useful to think of the same categories of responses as with papers. 1. Toss. Either actually delete the message, or ignore it. 2. Refer to someone else. Forward it to someone and take no further action. 3. Action, immediate. You do whatever you need to do right away, including replying to the email. 4. Action, deferred. You make an entry in your to do list to do whatever the message signals you to do; the entry will clue you as to how to find the original message. 5. File. Usually this means just leaving an email in your inbox, but sometimes it means copying and pasting it to another file. For text messages, sometimes this means emailing the message to yourself so that the message is on your computer rather than just your phone. For documents, this means putting them into a folder where it is logical to look for them, just as with paper folders.

What does the author advise doing with emails that need a response from you that you don't have time for right now?

A. Put a star by the email.

or
B. Make an entry in your to do list to do whatever the email requires.

Organizing computer files

165. Give some thought to how many folders you want to make on your hard drive or flash drive or place on the cloud. When do you want to have a subfolder for a subcategory under another, or when do you want to have a different folder at the same level? Are you able to find your computer files when you need them, without relying too strongly on memory? If the answer is no, give more thought to categories and subcategories. The basic idea, of course, is that all the information you have is divided into several sets, and some of those sets are further divided into subsets, and so forth. I recommend not having too many levels of folders -- it takes too long to get at the files if you do.

What's an example of what this text unit is referring to regarding folders and subfolders?

A. Having a folder for tax documents and a subfolder for each year that the tax is prepared.
or
B. Having a folder for billing and collecting and a separate folder for articles?

Organizing ideas

166. Most books that present ideas (in contrast to telling a story) are organized into chapters, sections of chapters, and often subsections of those sections. The chapters have titles with a style called "Heading 1," the sections with "Heading 2," the subsections with "Heading 3." A short article is usually still divided into parts, and each of those parts is often divided into subparts. Putting ideas into their logical place in such a division makes the ideas easier for the reader to understand. This also goes for spoken language, as well as written. If your speech is divided into topics, and you finish one topic before starting another, your ideas are easier to understand and remember. Conversely, if you randomly spout off ideas on one topic, then another, then another, then back to the first topic, and so forth, the ideas tend to confuse the listeners or readers. This is the reason why many of us were taught to make "outlines" of writing when in school. Even if you don't make outlines like those you see in English books, the principle of organizing ideas into parts and subparts is the same. And it is also the same as is used for the organization of computer files; this isn't surprising, because both consist of bits of information.

What's an example of the sort of organization of ideas this text unit is referring to?

A. In this book, the chapter titles are "Heading 1," the main divisions of chapters are labeled with "Heading 2," and sometimes there are subdivisions labeled with "Heading 3."
or
B. In a novel, the events are arranged in order of time, with the first events coming first, except for a few flashbacks.

Chapter 9: Reading people's cues

Five ways that people send you messages

167. One of the common characteristics of people on the autistic spectrum is difficulty picking up on the "cues," the messages, the communications that other people send. Again, this difficulty is shared by vast numbers of non-autistic folks. In the workplace, there are major advantages to being able to understand people's signals. If someone is sending a signal that says, "You're talking too long!" you want to pick up on it, and stop talking. If someone is sending a signal that says, "You're doing something inappropriate," you want to stop doing what you're doing and analyze the situation for future reference. If someone sends a signal that says, "I like what you're doing," you want to know it, so that you can feel good about that, and possibly do more of what you're doing.

What is one of the most important signals that people send, that you want to pick up on, mentioned in this text unit?

A. approval versus disapproval,
or
B. determination versus drifting?

168. The most obvious way that people try to communicate with you is by words,

spoken or written. But that's only one of the ways you get important signals from people. Here are the five big ones:

1. Words
2. Tones of voice
3. Facial expressions
4. Gestures or "body language"
5. Actions that send a message -- like giving a gift or destroying someone's property

Let's go into a little more detail about the second, third, and fourth of these.

This text unit implies that someone who gets the messages that other people send in words, written or spoken,

A. is doing all that is necessary to receive communications,
or
B. is missing out on the communications in tones, faces, gestures, and actions.

Tones of voice

169. Imagine someone speaking in a flat, monotone, emotionless voice. Even if the person's words say, "You did a good job on this," the utterance doesn't tend to make the listener feel nearly as good as would an utterance with more enthusiasm

and approval. We can call this "neutral" tones of voice.

Now imagine someone saying the same thing in a cheerful, more enthusiastic, perky, moderately excited tone of voice. "You did a good job on this!" We can call this "small to moderate approval." It feels much better to hear this.

Now imagine that the person is really astonished about how good the job was. "YOU did a GOOD JOB on this!!!!" The excitement is communicated by a big difference in pitch between the highest and lowest notes of the utterance. The words I put in all caps are spoken with a much higher pitch. We call this "large approval."

What's a point made in this text unit?

A. Speaking too loudly is not recommended.
or
B. The degree of enthusiasm and approval in a statement is roughly proportional to the pitch difference between the highest and lowest notes.

170. Interestingly, small to moderate disapproval and large disapproval have similar degrees of pitch difference to small to moderate approval and large approval, respectively. Imagine someone saying, "WHAT do you think you're DOING!!!!" with an angry look on the face and maybe slamming a fist down on a table. That's large disapproval. But the melody is rather similar to that of large approval: "WOW I can't believe how well you DID!!!!" The pitch difference signals excitement, and you can be excited in a positive or a negative way.

What's a summary of this text unit?

A. Large pitch differences signal excitement, and the melodies of large approval are very similar to those of large disapproval.
or
B. People tend to like other people in proportion to how much approval they get from them.

171. I want you to think about the degrees of approval or disapproval in the tones of voice that you use toward others, that others use toward you, and that other people use to each other. If you focus some attention on the degree of approval or disapproval you are sending, receiving, or observing, you will gradually gain two skills: the ability to regulate your own tones of voice so as to send the messages you want, and the ability to notice and read correctly the messages others send through tones of voice.

If you're in a training situation, here are some exercises to do with tones of voice:

1. The trainer says things with various degrees of approval and enthusiasm, and you identify which degree is being portrayed.

2. The trainer says things with various degrees of approval and enthusiasm, and you try to mimic the tones the trainer uses, as closely as possible.
3. The trainer gives you a phrase and a degree of approval, and you say the phrase with that degree of approval.

What's the purpose of this text unit?

A. to convince you that tones of approval are important.
or
B. to recommend observations and exercises that will help you pick up on others' degrees of approval or disapproval, and help you regulate the approval or disapproval in your own voice.

Facial expressions

172. What people are doing with their face muscles is often a strong clue to how they are feeling. Charles Darwin suggested that there is an innate language of emotion in facial expression that is fairly constant from one culture to the next; scientific work has since confirmed that idea, at least with respect to certain emotions like fear, surprise, happiness, disgust, sadness, and anger. Many more emotions than these can be conveyed by facial expressions.

What's a summary?

A. Some research has found that assuming certain facial expressions actually causes people to feel certain emotions.
or
B. Facial expressions provide a language that communicates emotion, no matter what language the person speaks.

173. If you're interested in sharpening your ability to read people's facial expressions, the Internet provides a great tool. Just type "facial expressions" or "facial expressions emotions" into your search engine, and look at the images that come up. You'll find lots of pictures of people's facial expressions, with labels for the emotions they are supposedly portraying. The quality of these vary, but by and large you can get lots of practice connecting up facial expressions with emotions by moving through these pictures.

Two basic signals you want to read accurately from people are approval and disapproval. I recommend typing "facial expressions disapproval" and "facial expressions approval" into your search engine and taking a look at what comes up.

Finally, I recommend paying attention to the facial expressions of the people you interact with. When they are using approving words or approving tones of voice, what do their faces look like? How about when they use irritated or worried words or tones of voice? I think you'll find that the range of facial expressions you see in the workplace provides less extreme examples of emotions than those you see on the Internet pictures. But the more you study them, the more sensitive you get to the more subtle facial expressions and what they mean.

What's the purpose of this text unit?

A. To trace some of the history of research on facial expressions.
or
B. To recommend some activities that will increase your ability to read facial expressions accurately.

Gestures or body language

174. If you type "body language" into your search engine, the images that come up purport to tell you the meaning of various body postures and movements. There are many exceptions to most rules that people have come up with to translate body language, so I would recommend not taking too seriously anyone who claims to have special insights into what people are communicating with their bodies. However, there are a few important ones. If you're speaking, and the listener ceases to look at you, and looks at his or her watch or the clock instead, you should at least entertain the hypothesis that the message is "I've heard enough from you," or "You're boring me." If you're speaking, and the listener takes out his or her phone

and starts reading or sending messages, you may have gotten the same message, only in a more rude way. (Be careful not to send this message yourself in this way!)

The author believes that

A. An expert in body language can read a person like a book.
or
B. Body language can be misinterpreted, but certain signals at least should raise the hypothesis that the person is thinking or feeling in a certain way.

175. If you're leaning toward a speaker, looking at the speaker's face, and nodding when significant points are made, the nonverbal message is, "I'm interested in what you're saying! I want to understand it!"

If someone physically moves away from you, on one occasion, this doesn't mean much. If someone consistently moves farther away from you, it could be that your sensory presentation is aversive, or it could be that you are in the habit of getting into what they consider their personal space.

What's a summary?

A. The signals that say, "I'm interested," and those that say "You're too close to me," are useful to read, and sometimes fairly obvious if you're paying attention to them.

or

B. Folding the arms across the chest has different meanings, or no meaning, and can't be read as meaning only one thing.

Try not to miss these messages

176. As you study tones of voice, facial expressions, and body language, try not to miss the following types of messages. They may provide very useful information for the workplace.

1. I'm listening; I'm tuned in; I'm glad to be doing so.

2. I'm focused on a task.

3. Someone's doing something inappropriate

4. Someone's talking too long

5. Someone's not tactful enough

6. I'm not interested in what's being said.

7. I need to get on with my work.

8. You joked, but I don't get it.

9. You said something, but I don't understand.

10. I appreciate your humor.

What's the purpose of this text unit?

A. To list some of the messages that you can get through tones, faces, and gestures, that are very much worth paying attention to.
or
B. To describe the tones of voice that are associated with each of several messages.

What if you're not sure?

177. There will likely be many times when you are not sure how to "read the cues." Even for people who are the most interpersonally sensitive, other people's tones of voice, facial expressions, and body language can be ambiguous. An important skill is knowing how to ask people to clarify their reactions, in a tactful way. If you're not sure what message someone is sending, you seldom want to communicate to the person that you have gotten a message that would be embarrassing for the other person to acknowledge. So here are ways, in my opinion, NOT to ask for clarification:

Why are you disapproving of me?
You look bored by what I'm saying, right?
I've offended you -- how have I done that?
You look like you don't like me bothering you. Is that right?
You looked at your watch, so maybe I'm talking to long for you -- is that it?

On the other hand, here ARE ways to ask for clarification:

I'm curious to hear your reaction to that, please.

If I'm talking too long, just feel free to interrupt or signal me somehow.

Did what I just said make sense to you?

I'm sometimes not too good at knowing what is appropriate -- am I breaking some social rules now, or am I doing OK?

Is this a moment that is OK to interrupt you, or should I come back a different time?

I hope what I said wasn't offensive?

What's the general difference between the ways to ask and the ways not to ask for clarification?

A. The "not recommended" ways may embarrass the other person by expressing a message you think you've gotten that is more blunt or insulting than the person wanted to send, whereas the "recommended" ways permit the person to give feedback in a way that is comfortable for the person.
or
B. The "not recommended" ways are unclear, whereas the "recommended" ways are more clear.

Chapter 10: Improving the Emotional Climate

The concept of emotional climate

178. In the interpersonal world of the workplace, or the family, or any other group, or even any relationship between two people, there is something called the *emotional climate*. In a negative emotional climate, people often

insult one another
criticize one another
boss each other around
contradict one another
threaten one another
make fun of one another
keep secrets from one another.
make each other feel bad

Whereas, in a positive emotional climate, people often:

compliment or otherwise approve of one another
listen carefully to one another
are assertive but tactful with each other when they disagree
help one another
teach one another
give to one another
do fun things with one another
try to console one another when bad things happen.

make each other feel good.

A good number of studies have found that positive emotional climates are good for people's mental health. The benefit is not limited to prevention or remediation of any one disorder -- the benefit occurs across the board.

What's a summary of this text unit?

A. In groups or relationships where people are nice to each other, the people tend to have better mental health.
or
B. In some groups, fellowship and fun are associated with substance abuse, and unsurprisingly, these groups have higher rates of addiction.

179. What goes into creating a positive or negative emotional climate can be very complex. The words and actions of the person in charge of a group, or the person who seems most powerful in the group, are very important in setting up an emotional climate. The amount of time pressure, the nature of the goals the group is striving for, and the personalities of all the individuals involved, among other factors, all contribute.

Despite this complexity, I find that any one person can usually unilaterally influence the emotional climate of the group or the relationship, simply by saying, with sincere enthusiasm, the following positive utterances.

What's a summary of this text unit?

A. Certain group members have more influence on the emotional climate than others, positive or negative.
or
B. The reasons for an emotional climate are complex, but even so, any one individual can influence the climate by saying the positive utterances listed below.

Things to say to improve the emotional climate

180. Here's a list of things to say if you want to try to improve an emotional climate.

Expressing gladness that the other person is here:

Good morning! Good afternoon! Good evening! I'm glad to see you! It's good to see you! Welcome home! Hi! I'm glad you're here!

Expressing gratitude and appreciation:

Thanks for doing that for me! I really appreciate what you did. I'm glad you told me that! Yes, please! That's nice of you to do that for me! This is a big help to me. Thanks for saying that!

Reinforcing a good performance of the other person:

You did a good job! That's interesting! Good going! Good point! Good job! Congratulations to you! You did well on that! That's pretty smart!

Positive feelings about the world and the things and events in it:

Wonderful! That's really great! Wow! Hooray! I'm so glad it happened like that! Sounds good! Look how beautiful that is!

Wishing well for the other person's future:

I hope you have a good day. Have a nice day! Good luck to you! I wish you the best on (the thing you're doing).

Offering help or accepting a request for help:

May I help you with that? I'd like to help you with that. I'll do that for you! I'm going to do this job so that you won't have to do it! Would you like me to show you how I do that? I'd be happy to do that for you! I'd love to help you in that way!

Positive feelings about one's own actions:

I feel good about something I did. Want to hear about it? Hooray, I'm glad I did this!

Being forgiving and tolerating frustration:

That's OK; don't worry about it. It's no problem. I can handle it. I can take it. It's not the end of the world.

Expressing interest in the other person:

How was your day today? How are you? How have you been doing? How have things been going? So let me see if I understand you right. You feel that _____. So in other words you're saying _____. I'd like to hear more about that! I'm curious about that. Tell me more. Uh huh . . . Yes . . . Oh?

Consoling the other person:

I'm sorry you had to go through that. I'm sorry that happened to you.

Apologizing or giving in:

I'm sorry I said that. I apologize for doing that. I think you're right about that. Upon thinking about it more, I've decided I was wrong. I'll go along with what you want on that.

Being assertive in a nice way:

Here's another option. Here's the option I would favor. An advantage of this plan

is . . . A disadvantage of that option is . . . Unfortunately I can't do it. I'd prefer not to. No, I'm sorry, I don't want to do that. It's very important that you do this.

Humor:

Saying or doing funny things, retelling funny things, or laughing when the other person is trying to entertain you by being funny. But avoiding sarcasm, making fun of the other person, macabre humor, or too sexualized or violent subjects for humor.

*   *   *

How would you characterize what these utterances have in common?

A. They tend to model positive emotion, be as pleasant as possible for the other person to hear, and to offer helpful actions.
or
B. They should all be spoken in a tone of voice of large approval.

181. I invite you to try an experiment. Get very familiar with these utterances. Look for appropriate opportunities to say them. Say them, with enthusiasm. Keep going for a good amount of time. Notice what effect there is upon the emotional climate. I think you'll find this a very worthwhile experiment, and I predict that you'll find the results positive.

The experiment the author proposes is to

A. Say the above things often, and see what happens to the emotional climate of the group or relationship you're in.
or
B. Try to persuade all the members of the group or relationship you are in to start saying things like those in the above list more often, and see what their reaction is.

Chapter 11: Decisions, Individual and Joint

182. When is the last time you made a decision? Probably a second or two ago, when you decided to read this rather than to stop reading. Some decisions are unconscious -- for example the decision you also made a few seconds ago to keep breathing rather than to stop. Like breathing, some decisions are "by default" -- i.e. something we do or not do automatically unless there a conscious decision to do otherwise -- such at the decision you probably also made a few seconds ago *not* to do push-ups while reading this sentence. But even those are still decisions -- brain activity about what to do and what not to do.

      These whimsical observations illustrate that life, at least the waking part of it, is an endless stream of decisions. We cannot avoid deciding. We can postpone or avoid deciding on certain choice points, but that in itself is a decision: "What I've decided to do is to figure out what to do, later, not now."

What's a summary of this text unit?

A. Every waking moment we are making decisions -- you can not avoid choosing what to do. Some choices involve more conscious thought than others.
or
B. A "choice point" is a situation we are in, where we have the chance to choose what to do, think, or feel.

183. We can define mental health as making, and enacting, decisions that tend to increase one's own long-term happiness and the long-term happiness of others. I find this thought comforting: no matter what has happened in the past, all we have to do is to make good decisions, one after another, to be mentally healthy.

What's a restatement of the idea the author finds comforting?

A. All human beings should be treated with dignity and respect.
or
B. If we can just make the best decisions we can, increased happiness of self and others is likely to ensue, despite whatever bad things happened in the past.

184. We'll talk about two types of decisions: individual and joint. In an individual decision, you are deciding what you yourself will do. In a joint decision, you are communicating with at least one other person about possible plans of action which will affect both (or all) of you. When I make an individual decision, the options are possible plans for *me*; for a joint decision, the options are possible plans for *us*. Someone hears a critical comment from someone and decides what (if anything) to say back: that's an individual decision. Two people

in a family are taking a vacation together and decide where to go: that's a joint decision. When one person wants one thing, and someone else wants something else, that's a special case of a joint decision known as interpersonal conflict. For example, two people ride in a car together; the driver prefers to go 80 miles per hour on a certain road and the passenger prefers a speed of 65 miles per hour. If they can figure out an option suitable to them both, we call that resolution of the conflict.

Two people have a problem with each other, in that the first tends to interrupt the other more than the second would like. But the first sees the second as almost always doing something, and the only way to start interacting is to interrupt. This situation is a typical one calling for

A. a joint decision,
or
B. an individual decision?

185. This entire book has been for the purpose of helping to make and enact better decisions. The chapter on social conversation has to do with decisions about when and how to talk and listen. The chapters on emotional regulation have to do with deciding how to act in situations that tend to bring out emotion. The chapter on organization has to do with decisions on how to keep things organized. And so forth. This chapter will go further into the general process of making individual and joint decisions, by outlining steps, or tasks, for both of those.

What's a summary of this text unit?

A. The field of decision science has identified certain types of errors that people seem to make frequently.
or
B. This whole book has been about making good decisions; the following sections will go into the general process of making individual and joint decisions.

Optimizing versus satisficing -- what are the stakes?

186. The steps I'm about to outline are for those choices that are "important," that are likely to make a difference in the happiness of yourself or someone else. I do NOT recommend going through these carefully for decisions such as:

I'm pulling into a parking lot: which of lots of empty parking spaces do I park in?
I'm buying a wood pencil. Do I get a red one or a yellow one?
Which socks do I put on this morning?
There are several healthy things to eat in my refrigerator -- which do I pick for lunch today?
Do I go to bed right away, or do I read for five minutes first?

For all these, one random choice is likely to be about as good as any other. The strategy of just picking the first option that is "good enough," without comparing all possible options, saves lots of time. The decision scientists call this "satisficing." On the other hand, choosing a career, choosing a spouse, choosing where to invest a lot of money, choosing whether to drink alcohol, choosing how to spend lots of time, and similar choice points are situations where the time taken to explore various options and try to pick the very best one will pay off. This way of deciding is called "optimizing." We ought to invest more time in optimizing, the higher the stakes of the decision.

What's a summary of this text unit?

A. Invest more time and thought into the decisions that are more important, and do the first thing that's good enough for the unimportant ones.
or
B. The way that we've seen other people act in similar choice points usually has an influence on how we choose to act.

Steps, or tasks, for individual decisions

187. Let's break the decision-making process into parts.

1. Situation. Understanding what is going on

Imagine that you were going to get advice from someone about what to do in a certain situation. You would have to give them a nutshell summary of what the situation was. But the quality of advice you would get would greatly depend on how well you described the situation -- how much you grasped the important elements of it, and described those, and didn't get bogged down in the details that aren't relevant to the decision. Exactly the same thing is true when you are presenting the situation to yourself rather than to an advisor. The better your narrative, in your own head, of what is going on, the better you're set to decide what to do.

What's a summary of this text unit?

A. Unless you know what it is that you are trying to maximize, or what outcomes you are trying to achieve, you don't have a basis for deciding.
or
B. A first step in deciding is becoming aware of the important aspects of the situation you're in, getting a good description and narration of your choice point.

188. For example, suppose someone's description of the choice point is: "I have too much work to do, in too little time."
Now imagine that the person fleshes out that description. "I was invited

to collaborate on a project with some coworkers. I think I'm making a good contribution to that project. But my supervisor assigned me another big task. I don't think he was aware that I was pretty busy on the first project. I think that I'm being expected to do two jobs at once."

The second description gives you better ideas about what to do about the situation, doesn't it?

Why is the second description better?

A. It tells the story of the events leading up to the situation, and these events give more of a clue about what to do about the situation.
or
B. It uses clearer language.

189. Here's a second example. Suppose the person's description of the choice point situation is: "A coworker is giving me mean looks."

Now imagine that the person fleshes out the description. "My coworker and I are in cubicles next to each other. When I'm working, I have a habit of automatically speaking aloud some of what's going on in my head. My coworker gives me irritated looks when I do that. But it's very difficult for me to change that habit, because I've been doing that for a very long time. The more I concentrate on what I'm doing, the less able I am to think about what I'm saying."

Again, the second description leaves you in a much better position to think of solutions to the problem, doesn't it?

In thinking about making your own situation descriptions for yourself, consider including:
1. All the characters who play a role in the story.
2. What the various people are wanting, what's at stake for them.
3. What the causal chains are -- what caused what to happen, and what the result of that was, and so forth. If you're not sure about causes, include that in the choice point description.
4. How often something happens, how long it happens, and how intensely it happens.
5. If you were giving advice on this situation, and someone described it to you, what questions would you want to know the answers to before giving advice?

What's the purpose of this text unit?

A. To inspire you about the importance of good decisions.
or
B. To illustrate and list some of the bits of information you should consider including in your narrative of the situation.

190. When you fully understand the situation you're in, you're in a good position to decide how high the stakes are. You can decide how much time to sink into the rest of the steps, or whether

to just satisfice by picking the first option that seems good enough, and moving on.

The author implies that

A. The decision about how much to satisfice or optimize comes before any of the steps of decision making.
or
B. You can best decide how much to satisfice or optimize only when you've become aware of the relevant aspects of the situation you're in.

2. Objectives

191. What sort of outcome are you trying to produce? If you know where you want to go, you're much more likely to get there!

As one example of choosing objectives: In provocation situations, where someone has done something that has made you angry, it is a natural reaction to automatically form the goal of getting revenge, or perhaps to teach the other person a lesson through punishing the person, or to get one's anger out so one will feel better. But these goals tend to lead people astray. Other goals lead to better outcomes -- goals such as resolving the conflict, making sure that one comes across as a reasonable person, figuring out the best solution to the problem, leaving the relationship in good standing, or avoiding a precedent of dominating the other person or being dominated. If you pick good objectives, you are more

poised to generate and select good options.

What's the main point of this text unit?

A. Getting revenge is not a good objective to have in provocation choice points.
or
B. Think carefully about what your objectives are, because these will determine what options are logical to generate and select.

3. Information

192. Suppose you have to decide which of two job offers to take. The more you know about both of the positions, the better you are able to decide. Of course there are the rate of pay and the official job descriptions, and the working hours. But you also want to find out as much as you can about the person you'll be reporting to -- what that person expects, whether the person communicates clearly, where the person falls on the kindness versus unkindness spectrum, and others. You also want to find out about the interpersonal climate of coworkers. If you have certain quirks and eccentricities, you want to find out how well these will be tolerated. If possible, you want to get a very clear picture of exactly what you will be doing, how fast, and how much. Is the business in good enough financial shape that there will not be layoffs soon? Do you need to relocate your residence for this job, and if so, there are many

questions about living in the new area that will be helpful to answer.

For this example, as well as many others, the task of getting information may be the most time-consuming, and also the most rewarding, of the decision process.

What's the main idea of this text unit?

A. In order to make a good choice about an option, it's often helpful to get lots of information with which to predict the consequences of the option, and lots of information about the situation in general.
or
B. Information technology has contributed a great deal to decision science. Algorithms for complex decisions can contribute when the complexity is too great to hold in mind.

4. Listing options

193. When faced with an important choice point, it's good to generate as many plausible options as possible before evaluating those options. Many people stop generating options after only one or two of them. But in order to enact the best decision, you first have to think of it. For very important decisions, it's good to actually write down the options.

Because the option-generating process is so important, part 2 of this book gives many situations that you can use to practice with. You are invited to generate your own options, and then

compare them with the ones I've generated.

For important decisions, the author recommends

A. generating two options to compare.
or
B. generating as many plausible options as you can think of?

5. Advantages and disadvantages

194. You judge an option by its predicted consequences -- you want to pick the option that will produce the best results. A positive consequence we call an advantage, and a negative consequence, a disadvantage. For the options that are highest on your list, you may want to write down the advantages and disadvantages you predict. Another phrase for advantages and disadvantages is pros and cons. The more information you've gathered, in a previous step, the more accurately you can predict consequences.

For each consequence you predict, you can also estimate how likely it is to occur. On a sunny day, it is possible to get struck by lightning, but this is a very unlikely consequence and not a big disadvantage for the option of being outside. When the sky is dark and there are thunder and lightning all around, the same consequence is a much bigger disadvantage because it is more likely.

Each advantage or disadvantage is more important depending upon how large the effect on your fortunes is. This is sometimes called the "utility" or "disutility" of the consequence. The possibility of getting killed by lightning is a much bigger disadvantage than the possibility of getting wet from rain, because the disutility is much higher.

What's an idea of this text unit?

A. How important an advantage or disadvantage is depends on both the probability of the consequence and its utility or disutility.
or
B. Some systems of thought evaluate options on bases other than their consequences.

6. Deciding

195. You somehow integrate all the information you've gathered, so as to make the choice. One way of doing this is to make an estimate of the "expected utility" for each option. The expected utility is a weighted sum, of how good or bad the result would be for each possible consequence of the option, weighted according to how likely that outcome is. For gambling situations, it's often possible to figure out the expected payoff of money. For example, suppose there are two lotteries. For one, there is a 50% chance of winning $100 and a 50% chance of winning nothing. For the

second, there is a 10% chance of winning $300, and a 90% chance of winning nothing. The "expected" payoff for the first is .5 times $100 plus .5 times $0, or $50. For the second, the expected payoff is .10 times $300 plus .90 times 0, or $30. So if you played the first option many times, you would average a payoff of $50; for the second, you would average $30. All other things equal, the first is the better option. But if it cost you $60 to buy a ticket for the first, and $35 to buy a ticket for the second, you would expect to lose $10 per game for the first and $5 a game for the second, Neither option would be worth doing in this case, but the second would in this case be preferable to the first.

In most situations in life, we are dealing with "happiness units" that are much harder to turn into numbers than the payoffs of gambling games. And the probabilities of different consequences are much more difficult to estimate. Still, the expected utility formula -- the sum of the happiness payoff of each consequence times the probability of that consequence, is a great mental device to use when evaluating options.

How do you use the expected utility formula?

A. For each option, list the possible consequences. Add up the products of the utility and the probability for each consequence. This gives the expected utility for that option. Do this for the

other options also, and the option with the highest expected utility wins, in this system.
or
B. List the advantages and disadvantages of each option, and pick the option that has the greatest number more advantages than disadvantages.

7. Doing what you have decided

196. Unfortunately, making a good decision is not the same as enacting it. If it were, millions of people who make new year's resolutions to get more exercise and eat a better diet would actually carry out those resolutions! Doing what you have resolved to do often requires the skill of self-discipline.

Which of the following is an example of a decision where the self-discipline to do what has been decided is the toughest part of the process?

A. Deciding which of two operative procedures to get, based on the risks and the benefits and the costs.
or
B. Someone decides to greatly reduce her intake of foods with sugar in them.

8. Learning from the experience

197. After you have enacted your decision, you see how well things worked out. Did the actual consequences match your predicted consequences? If not, would this experience help you in predicting consequences more accurately in future situations like this? You want to learn all you reasonably can, but at the same time you don't want to overgeneralize too much from one experience. Sometimes you need a decent "sample size" before you can conclude anything at all.

Which is a better summary of this text unit?

A. If an option is followed by a bad result, learn from the experience and never do that same option again.
or
B. You want to learn from your experiences, but it's important not to overgeneralize from an inadequate sample or to infer causality that doesn't exist.

Mnemonic: SOIL ADDLE

198. Situation, objectives, information, listing, advantages, deciding, doing, learning from experience -- when we put the first letters of these steps in order we get the phrase SOIL ADDLE. This may help you remember the steps of individual decision-making.

The second D in SOIL ADDLE stands for

A. deciding,

or

B. doing what was decided?

Steps, or tasks, in joint decision-making: Dr. L.W. Aap

199. Now we turn to joint decision-making, where two or more people have a conversation aimed at settling upon a course of action that affects them jointly. The following tasks or steps are characteristics of conversations that are meant to maximize mutual understanding and joint utility, and minimize threats and the use of coercion. The tasks are: defining, reflecting, listing, waiting, advantages, agreeing, and politeness. If you put the first letters of these together, you get the mnemonic for the 7 tasks of joint decision making: Dr. L.W. Aap. Let's examine each of these.

1. Defining the choice point

Defining the choice point (or the problem to solve) often is best phrased in a statement like,

"When X happens, it affects me in this way. Could we talk about what to do about that?"

Or perhaps, "There's something coming up, namely _____ that will affect us both.

Can we talk some about what we're going to do?"

Or even, "As I understand it, you would like for X to happen, while I would like Y to happen. Can we talk about what to do about this?"

In other words, you start the conversation trying not to accuse, insult, or command the other person or make the other person get defensive. It's better not to start the conversation by saying things like:

"Quit doing that thing! It's really a stupid thing to do!"

"Why do you always have to do that?"

"You need to do that."

"It's only right that you should do this thing that I want you to do."

"You are a _____," where the blank is filled in by a derogatory name.

What appear to be two purposes of the people's definition of the problem or choice point?

A. To get the problem onto the table for discussion, while avoiding making the other person feel attacked or accused or otherwise in need of self-defense.

or

B. To evaluate which option or set of options has the highest ratio of benefits to costs?

2. Reflecting

200. The second person, the one who hears the definition of the choice point, does a reflection to make sure that message is understood correctly. "So if I understand you correctly, the way you see the problem is ____."

After that, it's time for the second person to define the problem from his or her point of view. Then the first person does a reflection to make sure he or she understands correctly.

Thus both people tell their points of view, and both reflect the other's point of view. They may need to go back and forth like this for a while, seeking to understand how the other sees things and help the other understand their own viewpoint.

What do you imagine is the next step if the answer to the reflection is, "No, that's not what I meant?"

A. To go on to listing options regarding the problem.
or
B. For the person defining the problem to try again, and let the other person reflect again, until both people feel they have been understood.

3. Listing options

201. Once they understand each other's points of view, it is time for them both to participate in generating options. I think it's good for each person to mention at least two options, so that they don't become wedded to any one option.

4. Waiting until listing is finished before evaluating

When one person lists an option, the other person doesn't shoot it down and explain why it won't work -- at least not yet. They keep thinking of options until they run out. When they think they've generated enough ideas, they go on to the evaluation stage -- but not before then.

Why do you think the process involves waiting until the listing is over before evaluating the options?

A. In order that someone hearing the conversation can keep the various steps organized in mind.
or
B. So that the people will not get so sidetracked on arguing about which option is better, that they neglect thinking of an option that might be better still.

5. Advantages and Disadvantages

202. Once they've gotten some good options in mind, they talk about the advantages or disadvantages of the options -- not the good or bad traits of the other person!

When discussing an option, someone says, "If you were a decent person, you wouldn't even consider doing that." What's a translation that is more in keeping with what the author recommends?

A. People who advocate that idea have no place in this country.
or
B. A disadvantage of that option is that it would create fear in many people and do lots of harm thereby.

6. Agreeing

203. They agree on something, even if only to table the decision until later. Or perhaps they agree that the decision has to be settled by a court or some other authority, because they can't settle it themselves. Or they jointly decide that the more powerful person (for example a parent or boss) will settle the issue, with the protest of the less powerful having been noted. Ideally, they agree on an option or set of options that they have generated that constitutes a "win-win," a solution beneficial to both or all.

7. Politeness .

Throughout the whole conversation, they are polite with each other. That "includes but is not limited to": not raising the voice at the other, not insulting the other, not interrupting, being as tactful as possible.

Which of the two maxims below seem to be what the author advocates?

A. Let there be a struggle for dominance, and the strongest person gets their way.
or
B. Try to maximize the total happiness of both people, so that the agreement is based on voluntary action rather than coercion?

An example

204. Here's a quick example of what the process sounds like.

Person 1: May I talk with you about something? You have a habit of speaking aloud to yourself as you work, for example exclaiming out loud when something goes well or goes badly. Since we work so close to each other, I'm distracted by this. (defining)

Person 2: So my speaking aloud as I work is not pleasant for you. (reflecting)

Person 1: Right.

Person 2: Well my point of view is that I totally understand that my doing this is not a good habit. But I've tried changing it, and I just haven't succeeded yet. (defining)

Person 1: So you realize that the habit can be distracting, but it's hard to change. (reflecting)

Person 2: Correct.

Person 1: One option is that you could try other methods of habit change, like counting the number of times you do it, figuring out something else to do instead when you get the urge, and that sort of stuff -- there's a lot that's been written on habit change, and maybe some of it would help. (listing)

Person 2: Another option is that we could just see if the place where I work could be moved farther away from you. (listing and waiting)

Person 1: I could try some way of masking the sound or using headphones to keep it out. (listing and waiting)

Person 2: Another possibility is that you could try to get used to the sounds over time. (listing and waiting)

Person 1: Ready to start thinking of pros and cons?

Which of the steps in Dr. L.W. Aap have they done so far?

A. Dr. L.W.
or
B. Dr. L.W. Aa

205. The conversation continues.

Person 2: Yep. A disadvantage of headphones or earbuds is that you have to take them out or off each time someone talks with you. (advantages and disadvantages)

Person 1: Plus headphones aren't comfortable for me to wear for a long time. (advantages and disadvantages)

Person 2: I could try changing my habit, but a disadvantage is that this would take a lot of concentration and would be distracting for me, and I'm under a lot of pressure now to get a bunch of things accomplished. But an advantage is that it would make me get along better with anyone I worked near. (advantages and disadvantages)

Person 1: An advantage of moving one of us so that we're farther away from each other is that I believe there are several possible spaces that would work out. (advantages and disadvantages)

Person 2: That sounds like the best option for now. Want me to ask our supervisor about the move?

Person 1: That would be great. I'll let you know my ideas about possible places to move to. (agreeing on an option)

Person 2: Sounds good. Thanks for talking with me about this. (politeness)

Person 1: Thank you for being so reasonable about it. (politeness)

Since there were four options generated, someone might not remember who listed the option that was eventually chosen? If it's hard even for the participants to remember that, what positive effect do you think this might have?

A. The two people might be more able to judge the options on the basis of their advantages and disadvantages rather than thinking of them as "my way" and "your way."
or
B. The two people may be able to define the problem or choice point in ways that don't get the other person defensive.

But people don't talk like this in real life

206. The fact that people seldom are as polite and rational in real life as they are in the above conversation is not so much a criticism of the 7 tasks as a criticism of humanity. People have been known to kill each other over such issues as who gets to use a certain parking space. They scream at each other, cut off contact with each other, and spend years working on martial arts to defend themselves from each other. They get very angry and try to discharge their anger on other people, sometimes through mass acts of violence.

They also have rational, reasonable conversations without going through each of the 7 steps.

They particularly don't speak this way in movies and books. Entertainment thrives on conflict, and it is boring for most audiences to see and hear people being calm and rational and solving a problem fairly efficiently.

The relevant question is, would the world be better off if people did speak more like this? You can decide what you think about that!

In responding to the often-raised criticism that people in real life don't speak in this rational and polite and non-dominance-oriented way, the author argues that

A. They do speak in this way more often than is realized.
or
B. They should speak in this way more often than they do.

Part 2: Choice points

This part of the book is meant to give you practice at decision-making in choice points of the sort that occur in workplaces. My recommendation is to read the choice point, generate your own options for how to respond, and then compare your options with the sample options I have generated. Then, my recommendation is to think about the pros and cons of the options, and decide which you prefer. It is probably lots more fun to go through this process with someone else, and to generate options together and to either decide jointly or compare decisions about which option you think is best.

If you run into workplace situations that you think should be included in this part of the book, or good options you think I've left out, please let me know, at the email address given at the beginning of this book. The vision is that both parts of this book will be revised and improved as more experience accrues.

*   *   *

Schedule change

You've gotten into a routine at work that is comfortable for you. You find out that the daily schedule is going to change a lot: you're going to be doing the same work, but with a totally different schedule and in some different places. Imagine that changes like this are stressful for you.

Options:

You could talk with your supervisor and see how big a problem it would cause if you were to stick to your original schedule and location. It is possible that if you communicate how stressful the change is, you could keep with the original.

You could use fantasy rehearsal to adjust to the change in schedule and location, visualizing yourself in the new arrangement, and imagining yourself as relaxed and coping well.

You could communicate to your supervisor that changes like this are stressful to you, and that your productivity will probably be lower for while, during your adjustment period.

You could use muscle relaxation or other relaxation strategies when you are in the new arrangment.

You could be aware of your thoughts, practice the 12 thought exercise about the situation, and pick the thoughts most useful to you.

Noisy cubicle

You're working at a cubicle. There is quite a bit of noise around you -- people's conversations, machines turning on and off, and so forth. You find this quite irritating and distracting; it interferes greatly with your ability to be productive.

You could talk with your supervisor about moving to a less noisy place.

You could use ear plugs and/or noise cancelling headphones.

If there is music or other sound you find soothing to have on while you are working, you could play these recordings over the headphones.

You could try some relaxation strategies to help yourself not to be so stressed by the noise.

If you are trying hard not to pay attention to the noise, you might try being "mindful" of it but seeing if you can get work done anyway.

You can try to use thoughts that reinforce yourself for the work you get done despite distractions.

You can ask your supervisor about shifting your work hours so that you come in during times when the office is otherwise empty.

You can find out whether it's possible to telecommute for at least some of the time.

Attention wanders after time

After a certain number of hours of work, you find it hard to stay focused; your mind drifts to other things.

You could talk with your supervisor about whether it's possible to take half an hour or an hour off for exercise, relaxation, recreation, or whatever else helps you "recharge your batteries," then come back to work somewhat refreshed.

You could work a little longer or start earlier in exchange for this.

You could just reduce the total number of hours you get paid for in exchange for this.

Annoying lights

You are used to incandescent lights. You find that the fluorescent lights in your workplace seem to be very annoying and distracting to you.

You could talk with your supervisor about undoing the bulbs in the fluorescent lights that are most annoying.

You could bring in an incandescent lamp of your own to use in place of the fluorescent lights.

It could be that the fluorescent lights flicker because a bulb or something else needs to be replaced; you could ask that this problem be addressed.

You could try wearing yellow sunglasses while working.

Teasing perhaps?

A coworker says things with a smile and a laugh; you're not sure, but you think maybe the coworker is making fun of you or teasing you.

If the coworker does this in the presence of other people, you could in a private conversation with another coworker who sees it, ask for some help in understanding what the person's intent is.

You could just respond good-naturedly, with the theory that even if the person is making fun of you, it's a better strategy not to get upset.

You could communicate to the person himself your confusion over what the intent is, and ask for clarification.

If you don't think what the person is saying is funny, you can just give the person a puzzled look, without smiling.

You could just ignore the question of what the person's intent is, and try to have a pleasant conversation with this person or other people who are present.

Simplified explanations

People in your workplace know that you are on the autistic spectrum, and they seem to respond by trying to make explanations of things super simple, as if you weren't very smart.

You could thank them for their clear explanations, and focus your energy on doing and saying smart things that eventually demonstrate your intelligence.

You could patiently listen to the explanations, and focus your energy on doing and saying smart things that contribute to the organization's mission.

You could politely explain to the person or persons who do this that even though you are not as good at some things as other people are, your ability to understand directions is not impaired, and if they are going to special effort to make the explanations simple, they can save themselves that effort.

Criticism from supervisor

You get some criticism of your work by your supervisor.

You can relax your muscles or use any other relaxation method.

You can quickly do a little "not awfulizing" and "goal-setting."

You can say something like, "Thanks for pointing that out; that will be helpful."

You can say something like, "OK, I will have to do some more thinking and problem-solving about that."

You can say something like, "I think you're right, that's a place where there's room for improvement."

You can say something like, "Can you tell me more? Can you give me some examples? Can you say more about what I should be doing instead?"

You can do a reflection: "So if I understand you right, _____."

You can just listen silently.

You can explain the reason for what you've been doing.

If you think the criticism is really excessive or inappropriate or abusive, you can say so to your supervisor, immediately or after thinking about it.

If you think the criticism is excessive, inappropriate, or abusive, you can confer with any coworkers who are allies to see what they think.

If you think the criticism is excessive, inappropriate, or abusive, you can speak with someone else in the organization such as in the human resources department or wherever else abuses are reported.

You can figure out a program for yourself to improve in the area that you were criticized in, involving frequent reminders to yourself, fantasy rehearsals, and self-monitoring of how you're doing.

You can make an appointment with your supervisor for a certain date in the future to get feedback on whether you've been able to improve your performance by that time.

You can informally ask your supervisor for feedback on how you're doing from time to time.

Deadline looks impossible

You are asked to finish a project by a certain deadline. A few days before the deadline, you realize that the deadline can't be met -- there's too much more to do and not enough time.

You could ask to speak as soon as possible with your supervisor, or whoever set the deadline, or both, to explain why the deadline can't be met.

You can seek to understand how important it is that the work be done by a certain time -- is the deadline arbitrary, or set by some important constraint?

If you can't speak to your supervisor or whoever set the deadline, you can send emails or leave voice mails or other notifications -- the sooner the better.

If the deadline is super-important to make, you can work overtime to meet it.

You can try to increase your work efficiency to try to complete the project sooner.

You can suggest getting additional person-power on the project.

Work too easy

People at work know that you have a "disability" status. They are seeming to respond by assigning you too little work or too easy work.

You can just do the work quickly and well, and ask for your next assignments, demonstrating your capabilities without needing to say anything.

You can be patient and wait to see if the quantity and difficulty level picks up once people see your work output, having confidence that this usually is the case.

If the situation persists over time, you can have a conversation with your supervisor and explain that you think you are being underutilized.

You can do the work you are assigned, and in the extra time figure out useful work to do that you have not been assigned.

Coworker takes credit

You have collaborated with some other people on a project. In front of other people, one of the other people on the project appears to take the credit for work that you did.

You could let the person take credit at the time, without saying anything, while pondering your response.

If your supervisor was one of the ones who heard the person take credit, you could have a private conversation with your supervisor, explaining what your role was. You could say that you didn't want to embarrass the person by correcting the person in public, but you did want the supervisor to recognize the work that was yours.

You can talk with your supervisor about how, in the future, work can be credited to the person who actually did it -- for example by your quickly showing your work to the supervisor first.

If you want to be a little riskier, an option is that just when the person takes credit, you could say, in front of everyone else, "Hey, did anyone else help you with that work?"

If you want to be even riskier, you could say, in public, "The work that you are speaking about was work that I did 100% of." (Or whatever percent you did.)

Impending layoff

You hear from a coworker that the workplace is going to be downsizing, and some people are going to get laid off. You realize that it's possible that you might get laid off.

You could find out more from the coworker about the source and reliability of his or her information.

You could have a conversation with your supervisor (not revealing the source of your information, to avoid embarrassing your coworker) in which you try to find out whether there will actually be a downsizing or not.

You could research the availability of other jobs, just in case.

You could update your resume and think about references, just in case.

You could just relax and ignore this, and wait until something actually happens before worrying about it.

Uncertainty about your appraisal

You're not sure whether you're doing well on the job or not.

You could ask your supervisor for feedback.

You could ask any coworkers who are familiar with your work for feedback.

You could try to get clearer in your own mind what constitutes good performance, and try to measure your performance yourself.

You can keep your own records of your work output, and go over them with your supervisor to see how they measure up to expectations.

You can see if there is anything published about the standards for your job, and compare what you are doing to those standards.

You can just relax and do as well as you can, and assume that if you are not criticized, you must be doing well enough.

Disclose or not?

You're in a conversation with a coworker, and you're deciding whether or not to disclose that you are on the autistic spectrum.

You can just go ahead and disclose this to all people who are interested, without any shame or embarrassment, and with pride, and without deliberating in each particular case, on the theory that if you project an attitude of feeling good about yourself, other people will pick up on that and not think that the condition is something worthy of shame.

You can keep quiet about this, on the theory that your coworkers will sooner or later become familiar with your individual characteristics anyway, and direct observation gives a better picture of you than any label does.

You can make an individual decision based on how enlightened you believe this coworker is.

If you believe that this coworker is enlightened, but others are very prejudiced, you can avoid labelling yourself so as not to trust that the coworker will keep a secret.

You can just disclose freely, no matter what your prediction is of people's attitudes, and remind yourself that if there are enough negative consequences that result, you can take them up with a lawyer familiar with the Americans with Disabilities Act.

Chip in for baby?

A coworker has just had a baby, and a different coworker asks you to chip in little money toward a present for that coworker. Your thought is that maternity leave in itself is already generous, and you don't know the coworker who had the baby very well at all.

You could just fork over a little money on the theory that it's more trouble than it's worth to resist the workplace social customs.

You could ask the person what the expected range is, and think about how big a sacrifice it is to contribute something in that range.

If you are strapped for money and pinching pennies, you could tell that to the person who is asking, and say that you are afraid you will have to use your money for other things at this time.

If you are childless, you could be open about your feelings that maternity leave really already represents a transfer made from childless workers to workers who have children, and that you want to let that be enough.

Lunch together?

People at your work are in the habit of going to eat lunch together. When lunchtime comes, you are mentally fatigued and you think that having to pay attention to conversation and do the right thing in conversation would be painfully draining of energy.

You could just eat lunch by yourself.

You could take a break just before lunch, and relax/meditate, exercise, be alone, or do something else to "recharge your batteries" so as to be refreshed and prepared for some socialization.

You could take the first few minutes of the lunch break to recharge yourself, and join your colleagues after taking this time.

As an alternative to eating lunch with a group, you could invite one person at a time to eat lunch with you somewhere else.

As an alternative to socializing at lunch, you could invite a group of colleagues, or invite them one at a time, to do things with you at other times.

Irony from coworker

There's a coworker who very often uses irony, says the opposite of what is meant. For example, this person says, "Well, that's really nice," when he or she means, "That's really bad." The person says, "How are you liking our weekly fun and games," when he or she means, "I didn't like that weekly event at all, don't you agree how bad it is?" You have trouble

knowing when this person is saying what they mean and when they are playing around and using irony.

You could say to the person things like, "Can you indulge me for just a second -- I'm not too good at irony -- when you said, "That's really nice," you really meant the opposite, right? ... OK, thanks."

If you're not sure what the person means, you can just keep quiet and listen more, and maybe the person's subsequent speech will clarify it.

If it's not important to understand the person's attitude toward whatever the person is talking about, you can just let it go and not worry about it or try to decipher what the person means.

If it is important to understand the person's attitude, you can take your best guess and do a reflection to try to see if you understood correctly: for example, "If I understand you right, you really don't like the way this is done, and you want it corrected, is that accurate?"

If it is important to understand this person's attitudes, you could try to have a private conversation with the person in which you tell them that often you're not sure whether they are using irony or whether they actually mean what they say.

Did I make the person sad?

Someone appears to be feeling sad. You happen to worry that you might have caused the person to be feeling bad.

You could ask the person an open-ended question about how things are going for them, how they are feeling, and try to be a very empathic listener if they tell you anything about what's happening in their life.

You could search through your memory to see if there is anything you could have done to cause distress or mental pain, and if you can't find anything, try not to worry.

You could ask another coworker who knows that coworker if you are correct in thinking that the person looks sad, and ask if there is anything you could do to help.

No allies

You have been functioning OK in the workplace for a while, but you have no "allies" whom you feel you can count on.

Now that you are familiar with the people in the workplace, you could think about whom you would like to try to cultivate as an ally.

You could try asking someone for help on something or offering help to the other person.

You could have more social conversations with the person, making sure not to encroach too much on the person's time.

You could invite the potential ally to do something with you on non-work hours.

You could try to have mutually supportive conversations with the potential ally at lunchtime or other breaks.

You could just do your work and not worry about cultivating an ally.

Not liking group chats

There are situations at work where several workers chat with each other. Imagine that you don't particularly enjoy that and don't feel you are good at it.

You could just stay out of group social conversations, and not worry about the fact that you don't enjoy them.

You could look for opportunities to have one-to-one conversations with people instead of group conversations.

You could be like an anthropologist and observe the group conversations and how they are done. You could think about the categories of utterances that this book describes, and notice how they are used.

You can relax physically.

You can not worry about being quiet and reserved.

Empathy versus machine-talk

There's a conversation in which someone reports that a relative was hurt in a tractor accident. You happen to be very interested in tractors, and you are tempted to ask about what type of tractor it was, and to talk about different brands of tractors and which are best.

You can just resist the urge to talk about tractors.

You can say, "I'm so sorry to hear that."

You can say, "That's so sad. Would you like to tell me more about that?"

You can say, "That must be really upsetting. How is he (or she) doing now?"

Topic is unfamiliar

A couple of people are chatting with each other about a topic that you know nothing about, and are totally unfamiliar with. You are sitting or standing with them.

You could just listen, and learn something about something new.

You could zone out, and have some pleasant thoughts on your own.

You could join the conversation and ask them more about this topic, getting curious about it.

Urge to repeat

You are chatting with someone, and you find yourself starting to say over again something you've already said.

You could resist the impulse to repeat yourself.

You could just give a very quick summary of what you said before.

You could just stop yourself, in mid-sentence if you want, and say, "But I already told you that, so I won't go through it again."

Peer gives you jobs

A same-rank peer assigns you a task, and you have time to do it and return it to him. Then the same person starts assigning you more tasks.

You could check with your supervisor about what the protocol should be in determining what you do with your work time.

If you are busy, you can tell the person that you can't do it, and if you are not, you can do it.

You can suggest to the same-rank person that he or she go through your supervisor in assigning you tasks.

You could just tell the person that you get the work assignments from the supervisor and not from him or her, if that's what your supervisor tells you.

Chain of command

There is a problem at work that you have noticed, that you think requires pretty urgent action. You have the urge to report it to your boss's boss.

If it is very urgent, you could go ahead and report it to the first person in management that you can report it to.

You could resist the urge to report it to your boss's boss, and go "up the chain of command," and report it to your boss first.

You could send an email to all the people in the chain of command simultaneously, also sending a text to your supervisor.

"Would you mind?"

Your boss says to you, "Would you mind stopping what you're doing and working on this other thing for a bit? Unfortunately we're in a bit of a time crunch, and this second task is pretty urgent." You consider answering the question of "Would you mind" honestly,

and reporting that you would mind fairly much.

You can think just a bit more and realize that "Would you mind" is a polite way of saying, "Do it," and just stop what you're doing and work on the more urgent task.

You can make sure you understand by doing a reflection, saying something like, "It sounds like doing this second task is of higher priority right now than finishing what I'm doing, huh?"

"Hate you" meaning you're awesome

There's a problem that is puzzling for your coworkers, and someone asks you to help out. The answer is instantly clear to you, and you tell them. One of them looks in astonishment and says, "I just HATE people who can do things like that!" You are trying to figure out how to take this comment.

You can assume that the person is being funny by putting on a big show of feeling very jealous, but that he doesn't really hate you, in fact he is in an indirect way paying you a big compliment.

You can assume that this is an ironic compliment to your abilities, and just smile in response.

You can not worry about what exactly the person means, but you can feel good about your ability to solve the problem.

You can think that even if the person does feel jealous of you to the point of feeling hate, the best way to respond is to be nice in return, and just say something nice like, "I'm honored to have been asked to help out."

Interrupt the presenter?

Someone is giving a presentation, and no one is asking any questions. The speaker is moving right along quickly. You have the urge to interrupt to ask lots of questions that are coming to your mind, perhaps saying "Excuse me" first.

You can search through your memory as to whether the person asked people to please hold their questions to the end.

You can search through your memory about whether in similar presentations, the custom has been to hold questions to the end.

Instead of asking all the questions that have come to your mind, you could try to figure out which is the one that would be most helpful to all the audience members to have answered right away, and go ahead and ask it. You could notice whether people seem irritated by the interruption.

If you want to play it safe, you could wait until someone else asks a question.

Start all over with explanation?

You are giving an explanation of something to some coworkers. About halfway through, you are interrupted. You get the chance to gain the floor again, and you get the urge to start all over from the beginning.

You could resist the urge to start all over, and pick up just where you left off.

You could think about whether you perhaps were interrupted because you were too long-winded or because people weren't interested in what you were talking about. You consider just yielding the floor to other people.

You could ask, "I was explaining _____, should I continue or figure that I've said enough about that?"

You could just wait and see whether anyone asks you to continue.

An imaginary kill

You have a chance to solve a problem, and you do it with a great deal of technical skill. Someone says, "I would just KILL to be able to do that." You are trying to figure out how to take this comment.

You could assume that the person isn't really a murderer or willing to be a murderer.

You could assume that the person is paying you a compliment, by saying how strongly they wish they could do what you just did.

You could not worry about what the person meant exactly, but just feel good about solving the problem.

You could say something kind and humble, like "I'm glad to have been shown this problem, and I appreciate your listening to my thoughts on it."

Change the topic?

You are sitting with two people who are talking with each other about a certain topic that doesn't interest you. You have the urge to say, "Excuse me," and to interrupt and change the topic to something that is more interesting.

You can relax your muscles to help you feel more comfortable with not interrupting them, and resist the urge to interrupt.

You can listen to the conversation anyway, seeking to learn more about something that is outside your interest area, to expand your interests.

You can every once in a while ask a follow-up question or do a reflection to check your understanding or try to understand more the topic they are talking about.

You can just silently wait until the topic of conversation comes around to something different.

Coworker's family member ill

In a conversation, someone reports that a family member was recently diagnosed as having a really bad illness. You're wondering what to say and do.

You can say, "I'm sorry to hear that."

You can say, "Would you like to tell me more about what people think will happen?"

You can say, "That must be really upsetting for you and the rest of your family."

You can say, "Do you feel confident in the doctors who are helping take care of it?"

You can say, "Oh, that's bad news. Would you like to tell me more about it?"

You can later on give the person a card expressing good wishes for their relative.

You can ask if there's anything you can do to help out in this hard time.

If you know the person well, you can consider visiting at the hospital, if the relative is in the hospital.

Bosses are arguing

Your boss and your boss's boss are having a conversation that sounds like an argument to you, and your boss's boss is criticizing your boss. You consider jumping into the conversation to defend your boss. What would be best to do?

You can just resist the urge to jump in to the conversation, especially if you are not officially part of the conference.

If you are just overhearing the conversation, you can move farther away so that the two of them can speak in privacy.

If you are overhearing the conversation, you can just listen silently and learn whatever you can that might be useful in understanding your workplace.

If you are officially part of the conversation, you can wait until one of the two of them looks at you and signals in that way that your input is desired. If you get this signal but aren't sure of it, you can ask, "Are you wanting to hear my thoughts, or shall I let the two of you continue?"

If you do get a signal to talk, you can speak in terms of facts that bolster the conclusions you want, rather than speaking opinions and wishes.

Minor correction

You do some work, and your boss is generally satisfied with it, but points out to you a minor correction that needs to occur in one little part. What do you say to yourself?

You could say to yourself, "Hooray, looks like about 99% of what I did is satisfactory! I did a good job!" (celebrating your own choice)

You could say to yourself, "I'm glad my boss communicated his general satisfaction, rather than giving the correction only. (celebrating someone else's choice)

You could say to yourself, "I'm glad my boss caught a little error. That helps make my output better." (celebrating someone else's choice)

You could say to yourself, "OK, I understand how I made that little error, and now I know how not to make it next time!" (learning from the experience)

You could say to yourself, "My goal is to be gracious and rational in this situation." (goal-setting)

You could say to yourself, "I could just go correct the mistake without saying anything. or I could say to my boss, 'Thanks for pointing that out. And thanks for your kind words about the rest of it. I'm going to choose the second.'" (Listing options and choosing)

You could say to yourself, "Everyone makes minor mistakes; this is not terrible." (not awfulizing)

Correcting the emailer

You get an email that was sent to a group of people. You have something to say that is a correction to part of what the sender said. You consider the question of whether to "reply all" or reply just to the sender and leave everyone else out.

You could just reply to the sender, so that the correction wouldn't embarrass the sender in front of everyone else the email was addressed to.

You could decide how important it is that the other people receiving the email be notified of the correction, and if it is not important, leave them out of your reply.

Even if it is important that the other receivers of the email be notified of the correction, you could still send it just to the sender, and let the sender have the chance to tell everyone else rather than your doing so; that way the sender saves face.

If it is important for all the receivers of the email to know of the correction, you could first send it to the sender only, wait a while, maybe check with the sender, and if all else fails send the correction out yourself.

Nervous smile

Imagine that you have realized that you often smile when you are nervous or don't know what to do or just are with people. Someone tells you about something sad that happened to that person. What do you think to yourself?

You could think, "My goal is not to give my nervous smile now, because I don't want to seem like I'm happy over the other person's misfortune."

You could think, "I want my facial expression to communicate that I'm concerned and compassionate."

You could purposely give a concerned and compassionate look, without smiling.

Unwanted job assignment

A fairly new boss gets assigned. This boss asks you to fill in for a couple of months for another worker who is on leave. The job is dealing with customer complaints. Imagine that the prospect of being in this job, of dealing with one dissatisfied customer after another, fills you with dread and you think you would be very bad at this job.

You could request a conference with the boss, and explain what your strengths and weaknesses are, and explain that the customer complaint department calls upon skills that are your major weaknesses. You can make a very strong request that someone more suited for this job be chosen to fill it.

If after you've told the boss that this is an area of weakness for you, if you're still assigned to fill this post, you can study carefully the types of responses that people are supposed to make to customers' complaints, memorize them, and just try seeing how it goes.

If you think the job would be way too stressful even for a couple of months, you could refer to being on the autism spectrum and make the case that assigning you to this task would be inappropriate for your disability status.

Wish to help criticized coworker

Someone at work has made a presentation, and several people are very critical of the person, in ways that you disagree with. You can see that the person feels bad, and you want to make the person feel better.

At the presentation, you can think of some valuable point that the person made during the presentation and comment on it in a positive way.

At the presentation, you can politely disagree with the critics, backing up your points with evidence and rationality as much as possible.

After the presentation, you can compliment the person on the presentation.

After the presentation, you can remark to the person about why the critics were too critical.

You could invite the person to talk about what happened, and just be a good and supportive listener.

You could say to the person, after the presentation, "I thought the critics were incorrect and too harsh." If the person talks about the experience, you could be a good listener.

You could just get together with the person and socialize, not mentioning the presentation unless the person brings it up.

Urge to keep questioning

You get a job assignment that makes you feel anxious about whether you can do it. You ask a question and it is answered, and you notice in yourself the urge to keep asking questions just to reduce the anxiety.

You could resist the urge to ask repeated questions until you have had a chance to sit down and analyze what you really need to know that hasn't already been communicated.

You could thank the person who answered the question, and then contemplate what you really don't know and need to ask in addition.

You could relax your muscles or use any other relaxation/meditation technique to reduce your anxiety.

You could become aware of your thoughts, and pick your thoughts so as to reduce anxiety.

You could study very carefully any manuals that have been written that describe how to carry out the new duties that you will have.

Greeted but you don't know name

Someone at work says hi to you, and uses your name. You realize you don't remember this person's name.

You could just return the greeting in an enthusiastic way, without using the person's name -- for example by saying, "Hello! How are you today!"

You could later on figure out the person's name by getting a list of names of people in your workplace, and looking for a picture of each, on the Internet if there's not one available at work.

You could later on figure out the person's name without having to ask the person, for example by looking at names on doors or on desks, looking unobtrusively at the person's name tag, looking at mail slots and using the process of elimination, and so forth.

You could later on ask someone else what the person's name is.

You could, after returning the greeting ritual without using the person's name, and searching unsuccessfully for a name on an ID tag, just say to the person, "I'm sorry, I'm not the greatest at remembering names, could you remind me what yours is?"

You could, without apologizing, after returning the greeting, say, "Please remind me of what your name is."

Discussion not directly relevant

There is a meeting you are in, where there is lots of animated discussion about some issues that don't directly affect what you should do. You wonder how to best use your time.

You could just listen, hoping to learn more about how the business works.

If there is animated discussion, some people must have some strong feelings about what should be done. You can listen with the purpose of understanding where people at work stand on various issues and who feels strongly about what.

You can listen and analyze how people make their points and how they are either convincing or not convincing in doing so.

You can let your mind drift onto other things; for example you can use the time to think about the decisions that you are facing at work now.

You can use the time to relax and feel peaceful that you don't have to really do anything about the issues being discussed.

You can tune in enough to carefully consider whether what is being said affects you, rather than having total confidence in your first judgment.

Boss neither all good nor all bad

You have a boss, and you are not sure whether the person is a good person or a bad person. The boss has done some mean things, but also has done some nice things.

You can get used to the fact that almost all bosses, and almost all people, do a mixture of good and bad things, and that people don't need to have a track record of 100% good decisions before you can form an alliance with them that is useful to you.

You can use writing to help you evaluate your situation. Sometime when you are not at work, you can make a list of the good and bad things the boss has done. You can ask yourself how good or bad each one is, particularly how bad the bad things are. Depending on how bad the bad things are, you can decide how much you want to trust this boss, or you may want to even seek a transfer or a new job.

When you think about the good and bad things, you can weight them more heavily depending on how recent they are. For example, if the boss made a really bad decision 20 years ago, that isn't as important as if it happened 2 months ago.

Urge to moralize

Someone describes a certain strategy for doing something at work. You think a different strategy has advantages. You notice yourself thinking and feeling that the strategy the other person has advocated is immoral, bad, evil.

You may want to take your time thinking about how you want to communicate about this, rather than composing your response right on the spot.

You may want to say, "I have some thoughts about this, but I want to think about this some more before talking about it more. I want to get my thoughts more organized first."

You can examine your own thinking and make sure that you aren't mixing up something that you think just wouldn't work as well, with something wrong and bad. You can think in terms of how much good or harm to human beings is at stake, and if the answer is not much at all, try to reduce the moralistic thinking.

You may want to argue against the strategy on the basis of the predicted consequences -- "This strategy could have this negative outcome, and I think the likelihood of that effect happening is this much." In other words, you might want to keep the words immoral, bad, evil, wrong, etc. out of your argument so as to avoid making the other person defensive and angry.

If after consideration you do think what is proposed is immoral, you might want to consult with other trusted people to see if they back up your opinion.

You may want to do research on the Internet or otherwise to get more information about the ethics involved.

You may want to consult a lawyer about the legality involved.

If after consideration you do think what is being proposed is immoral and unethical, one option is to speak to your supervisor about it rather than, or in addition to, speaking to the person who proposed it.

If after careful thought you do think that there is a moral and ethical issue at stake, you might want to explicitly say this, but in a calm and rational voice: for example, "I believe that there are serious ethical problems with what is being proposed."

If what is proposed looks like it is going to be enacted, and you have serious enough ethical problems with it, you may want to talk to as many people in the business as you can to persuade them, or resign your post in protest.

Routines to be upset by move

You have a place to work where you have gotten into a routine of looking out the window every so often. You find out that your work station will be moved, and your routine of looking over a certain shoulder to gaze out the window will no longer work. Lots of other little routines will also broken up by the move. You happen to find your work and your mood much more disrupted by changes like this than most people's are.

You could find out from your supervisor or others if it's possible, or how much trouble it would cause, to let you stay where you are.

You could look at the new place before the change is made and start using fantasy rehearsals to get used to the new location.

You could arrange that your own materials and props are put up in the same configuration after the move as before, and focus attention on them to keep things the same.

You could plan ahead to get as much work done before the move so that you can be a little easy on yourself if you are not as productive, and spend some more time just relaxing in to the change, for the first few days after the change.

When the change takes place, you can spend some time relaxing your muscles or using any other relaxation technique.

You can do the 12 thought exercise to prepare for the move.

When the move takes place, you can be aware of your thoughts, and try to revise any of them that seem to be producing worse feelings than you want.

Coworker catches on slowly

You are working with a coworker on a project. This person isn't nearly as quick at catching on to what you're doing as you are. The person keeps asking you to explain and justify things that you think the person should be able to pick up lots more quickly.

You can be patient and calm while explaining, as clearly as you can, anything that the coworker wants to have explained.

You can do the 12 thought exercise and come up with some good ways of thinking about the situation that help you feel good rather than bad. For example: You can celebrate luck, or celebrate your own choices, that you can pick up this material faster than the other person.

You can celebrate each of your choices to be patient and calm.

You can do goal-setting regarding establishing a good relationship with this coworker, and establishing a reputation as a good person to work with.

You can list options and choose regarding how to explain things most effectively.

You can not awfulize about any time spent in this venture.

You can not blame the other person for needing more time to catch on.

If there are written manuals that explain things really well, you can furnish those for your coworker in a spirit of helpfulness.

Boss criticizes part of your output

You work on a project, and show a version of it to a supervisor, who criticizes part of it. You have to decide whether to scrap the whole thing and start over.

You just think for a while about whether modifying things to take care of the supervisor's corrective feedback would make it necessary to scrap the rest of the plans you made.

You make a draft of the project with most of it still intact but the criticized part revised, and just see what it looks like.

You try to not awfulize and not get down on yourself about the criticism, but to learn from the experience, and if the criticism is constructive and helpful, even to celebrate luck and celebrate someone else's choice, that the supervisor improved things.

If the part that was criticized really is important enough to start all over, you can just do that without awfulizing about that, and try to be as efficient as you can.

Urge to correct, but new task

You recognize an imperfection in something you've done, and feel a very strong wish to correct it right away. But your supervisor has assigned a task to you that is of a good bit higher priority.

You can use a written to do list, with the to dos numbered in order of priority, to keep track of what you want to do an in what order.

You can just work on the highest priority task, and let the lower priority task ride for a while, realizing that there is usually more on the to do list than can be done right away.

You can let the supervisor know about the error that needs to be corrected, so that the prior project won't be used until the correction takes place.

If the error in what you have done really bugs you, and especially if it can be corrected quickly, you can correct it on your own time before or after work, just to get it off your mind.

If it can be corrected fairly quickly, you can just go ahead and do it, and then move forward full steam ahead on the high priority task.

Puzzling idioms

At work, people often use idioms like: "The ball is in your court," "Don't beat around the bush," "He's bitten off more than he can chew," "Are we on the same wavelength?" "I want to pick your brain," "Would you bring me up to speed," and so forth. Imagine that you find many of these hard to understand.

You can search on the Internet for a guide to idioms, (such as that found at https://americanenglish.state.gov/files/ae/resource_files/in_the_loop_pages.pdf) and just study these in your spare time.

If someone uses an expression that you don't understand, you could say, "I'm sorry, I'm not too good at understanding idioms or metaphorical language -- could you explain what you mean by that?"

You could try to remember what the person said, and then search for that particular phrase on the Internet and find an explanation of it.

If what the person is saying is not very important, you could just not worry about your failure to understand the phrase, and move on.

Vague directions

Your supervisor sometimes gives you vague directions. For example, "Do that later," without saying when it should be done by. Or "Just clean it up a bit and it'll be OK," when you don't know what is meant by "clean it up."

You could ask follow up questions to clarify. For example, "When should it be finished?" or "Can you explain to me what you mean by 'clean it up'?"

You can use your own judgment about how and when the job should be done.

You can try to understand the goals and processes of the whole organization more, so that your own judgment will be more accurate -- in other words, you learn to think more like a supervisor yourself.

You can ask a coworker ally for advice on how to interpret the vague directions.

Productivity unnoticed

You do lots of good work, but it appears to you that no one notices your productivity.

You could keep your own log of what you have accomplished, and just try to feel good about it independent of what other people think.

You could keep your own log of accomplishments, and every once in a while send it, or a brief summary of it, to your supervisor.

You could see if a coworker who is an ally would be willing to engage in mutual celebration of each other's accomplishments, either using a written log or just speaking from memory.

Coworkers in recreational pursuits

There are some people at work who spend a good bit of time in non work-related activities, such as playing a game with each other, looking up things on the Internet, and political activities. You wonder how to respond to this.

If you are invited or get the chance to be included in these activities, you could decline, out of concern that too much of such activities might result in people's getting fired.

You could resist any urge to report these people's activities to supervisors, on the grounds that this is the supervisor's duty and not yours.

You could resist any urge to report these activities to supervisors on the grounds that if they manage to produce enough good work despite their recreational activities, the supervisors may not care.

You could speak with a coworker who is an ally and ask about what the culture of the workplace is regarding activities like these.

You could in a conversation with a supervisor, without naming people's names or even mentioning that people are doing these, ask what the culture of the workplace is about activities like these.

What to wear

There is no official dress code where you work. You are wondering what you should wear, and how important what you wear is.

At the time you are hired, you could ask whoever hires you how important what you wear is, and what you should wear.

You could ask these questions of your supervisor.

You could just notice what your coworkers wear and wear clothes at least that dressed up, if not a little more so.

You could make sure to wear clothes that are clean, no matter what the customs are.

On task versus socializing

You try to keep on task at work, and not waste time in idle chatter. But you wonder if you are being negatively judged for sticking too much to yourself and not getting to know your coworkers.

You could just do your work and not worry about whether you are sticking too much to yourself, taking your own good time about getting to know people.

You could think about which ways of getting to know coworkers are most comfortable for you: joining groups, chatting with someone one-to-one, getting together with a coworker after work, and do whatever you are comfortable with.

You could ask a supervisor or coworker to advise you on how important it is to form relationships with coworkers.

Fatigue from social interaction

You find that navigating social interactions gets you very fatigued, and you need to recover by being alone for a good while.

If your job consists of some activities that you do with people and some that you do alone, and the balance is too far in the direction of social activities, you could talk with your supervisor about the possibility of altering the distribution of your duties.

You could just take some "solitude breaks" in between rounds of dealing with people.

You could talk with your supervisor about "solitude breaks" and explain that these are really necessary for you to be able to navigate the social interactions successfully.

You could try to gradually desensitize yourself to the stress of social interactions, trying to relax your muscles, and trying if possible to start with lower

amounts and work your way up to tolerating higher amounts.

If worse comes to worse you could look for a different job where you do more alone work and less social interaction work.

The forest for the trees

Someone criticizes you with constructive intent, saying that "You have trouble seeing the forest for the trees."

Options regarding how to reply to the person at the moment:

You could say, "So if I understand you right, I get so wrapped up in the details sometimes that I lose track of the overall goal?" (Reflection)

You could say, "You're trying to help me perform better by telling me that, and I appreciate your doing so." (Thank you.)

You could say, "OK, I will think about that, and what I can do about it." (Planning to ponder or problem-solve.)

You could say, "Can you tell me more about that, maybe with some examples?" (Asking for more specific criticism)

You could say, "You're right, I'm pretty detail-oriented, that's true." (Agreeing with part of criticism)

You could say, "Yes, but I still think this detail is important and should be addressed." (I want statement.)

Options regarding how to respond afterwards:

You could self-monitor times when you get so bogged down in little things that you lose sight of the larger issues or overall goals.

If you find that there are lots of times when you do that, you can celebrate the opportunity to improve things by often re-orienting yourself to the question of what the overall goal and plan is.

If you find that there are not many times when you do that, you can celebrate the fact that the criticism you got is not very valid.

You could ask for feedback from other people, e.g. supervisor or coworker ally, about whether this criticism is valid and important.

You could monitor more closely your overall work performance and productivity, and if they are good, celebrate.

You find yourself procrastinating

Imagine that you have some tasks at work that are particularly unpleasant, and you tend to put them off.

You could do fantasy rehearsals of getting the unpleasant tasks out of the way and feeling really good about yourself for doing so, and then trying to enact these imagined patterns.

You could just resolve to get them out of the way, try to keep your resolution, and celebrate greatly when you succeed.

You could keep in mind the concept of "shaping": rewarding yourself not just for the completion of the goal, but for many of the steps toward it, just by saying to yourself, "Hooray, I've made another bit of progress!"

You could figure out some tangible rewards, like something you want to buy or eat or do, and withhold them from yourself until you get the unpleasant tasks done.

You could arrange with someone else to withhold some tangible rewards from yourself until you get the tasks done.

Focusing versus multitasking

You have a job that requires you to focus intensely on one thing for quite a while, and you are good at this. Your supervisor wants to switch you to a position where you have to do a lot of multitasking and shifting gears between one task and another. Imagine that you find it particularly hard to "transition" from one task to another.

You could ask for a private conference with your supervisor, and explain that you are good at some things and not at others.

You could explain that the organization would best use your talents by assigning you to tasks that require hyperfocus and avoid assigning you to the ones requiring multitasking.

You could instead of having a private conference, write an email to your supervisor explaining this.

If you believe that the change would be really bad for your job performance and job satisfaction, you could speak with someone in the disabilities office of your workplace, if your job has such.

You could work on the art of shifting focus from one task to another, using something other than the new position to practice, and see if it is possible to improve at that skill.

If you let your supervisor know that you think that your taking on the new position would be a bad idea but you are given no choice, you could try it out for a while to gather first hand information rather than trying to predict without that experience.

If worse comes to worst, you can look for a different job that will use your abilities to focus in ways that are more suited to you.

Agenda temporarily empty

You have finished a big, important task, and there is nothing on your agenda at the time being. You wonder what to do with your work time at the present.

You could check ahead of time with your supervisor whether it is consistent with the workplace culture that when the big task is finished, you can take some work time to celebrate its completion, perhaps with whoever collaborated with you.

You could just take a break, right at your work station, and celebrate in your own mind the completion of the task.

You could go outside or somewhere else off the work site and take a little time to celebrate.

You could do some routine organizing tasks while taking it easy for a while.

You could find out what the next item on the to do list is, and jump right into it without much of a pause.

Increasing upset feelings

You find yourself reacting to a situation at work by feeling more and more upset.

If the situation is working with someone else who upsets you, you could ask your supervisor about not having to work with that person, at least for a while.

If the situation is a particular task that is frustrating, you could ask your supervisor about switching to a different task, at least for a while.

If the situation is too much to do in too little time, you could explain to your supervisor the time requirements of the task and see if you can allot more time to the task.

You can just leave the work station and go out for a walk to cool off a bit. If appropriate, you can tell someone, e.g. your supervisor, that you are going to do this.

You can use a relaxation technique right on the spot.

You can observe your own cognitions and mentally do the 12 thought exercise. You can pick ways of looking at the situation that make it not so upsetting.

If the situation involves skills that are in short supply for you, you can work on those skills.

Your movements look unusual

Imagine that you have a habit of making some repetitive movements with your hands and arms that look unusual to other people when you do these at work.

If this is a long-term habit that you don't think can be changed any time soon, you can explain this to selected people.

You can explain that this is something that often goes along with being on the autistic spectrum, and it's just a harmless way of discharging energy or increasing the level of energy or getting stimulation, etc.

You can just not worry about this, and not bother explaining it.

You can, if you choose, work on changing the habit by picking something else -- a less obtrusive movement, a relaxation of the muscles, for example -- and practicing doing that each time you get the urge to do the more obvious movement.

Being efficient enough?

You worry that you are not working efficiently enough.

You could keep a log of what you do accomplish, over time. You could go over this with your supervisor and ask for feedback on how good the efficiency (or productivity per unit time) is, compared with what is expected of you.

You could keep a log of your accomplishments over time, and talk with a coworker who is an ally about whether the efficiency is good enough.

You could simply work at a level of speed that is comfortable for you and compatible with quality work, and not worry about it unless you hear that there's a problem.

You could search on the Internet and find out if there is anything published about productivity standards for your job.

Dreaded retreat

There is going to be a corporate team-building retreat, where the agenda is to do ice-breakers, play games, have teams do various challenges, do improvisational acting, talk about yourself to the rest of the group, have trivia contests, and so forth. Imagine that you've had a little experience with this sort of thing, which was very unpleasant, and the very thought of taking part in this creates terror in you.

You talk with your supervisor about this, and communicate that this sort of thing is extremely unpleasant, and that you would strongly prefer not to go.

You can talk with someone in the disabilities office first, and ask that being excused from things like this become an official accommodation for you.

You can simply not show up at the retreat, but show up at the ordinary workplace if you can, and work on your ordinary work.

You could ask to be able to go to the retreat but to just observe the activities but not to take part in them.

You could put on your long-term goals list getting more comfortable with these sorts of activities.

You could put on your long-term goals list being so productive in the workplace that you have a great deal of leverage in refusing to do things like this.

Obstacle for project

You are working on a project, but you come to an obstacle that you don't see how to get around.

You could consult with your supervisor about how to overcome the obstacle.

You could consult with a coworker.

You could consult with someone outside the organization.

You could look up the problem on the Internet and see if you can find an answer to the obstacle.

You could put the project aside for a while and let the problem incubate in your mind and see if that makes it easier to devise a solution.

You could relax and realize that obstacles are the rule and not the exception in almost all projects, and let that thought help you to not awfulize.

If the obstacle is too big and too insurmountable, it is possible that the project would have to be abandoned. You would usually have to discuss this with your supervisor.

Party isn't fun

There is a little party at work. There is music playing, a lot of loud talking, and many conversations going on around you at once. Imagine that it so happens that this sort of environment is very aversive for you.

You could simply skip this event.

You could continue working in your usual workplace, if it is away from the noise.

You could take the time off by yourself, and go for a walk, or go home, or do anything else you want.

You might try hanging out far away enough from the noise that it doesn't bother you, and seeing if there is anyone who would like to get into a fun conversation with you.

Coworkers linger at lunch

There is a group of coworkers who get lunch together, and they welcome you into the group, and you enjoy being with them. But they tend to stay at lunch past the time when you're supposed to get back on the job.

You could go with them, but just excuse yourself so as to get back on time.

You could ask your supervisor how important it is to get back from lunch on time.

You could eat lunch with other people.

You could eat lunch by yourself.

You could talk with your supervisor about taking a little longer lunch and in return staying longer in the evening or coming in earlier in the morning.

You could ask a trusted coworker how important it is to get back from lunch on time.

Pressure to eat

Someone at work has brought in something for people to eat. You don't want any, but the person keeps pressuring you to have some.

When the person keeps pressuring, you can simply keep politely declining.

You can take whatever it is in order to take it home with you. When you get home, you can throw it away, give it to someone else, or do whatever else you want to with it.

You can, if you want, explain to the person why you don't want it. For example, "I stay away from dairy products because I get this strange reaction to them -- they seem to bother my skin and joints." Or "I'm unfortunately one of those rare people who just doesn't like chocolate."

Solution to overheard problem

You overhear two coworkers puzzling over a technical problem. You think up a solution to their problem that you are rather sure will work well.

You can just pretend you didn't hear and stay out of it.

You can say to one or both of them, "I couldn't help overhearing the problem you were puzzling over, and I think I know how to solve it. Would you like to hear my idea?"

You could say to them, "Excuse me, would you mind if I joined your conversation? I think I can help with what you're talking about."

You could give them some time to work on it by themselves, and offer to help later on it they still are perplexed.

Index

advantages and disadvantages.....107, 112
allies...35
Americans with Disabilities Act............13
anger...18
anger control.......................................37
anger control program..........................49
anxiety reduction..................................54
appointment calendar............................87
appointment-keeping.............................15
autism, meaning of................................11
aversion reduction, summary................64
aversions..54
away from the other, in anger..............38
biofeedback...44
body language......................................95
bosses, relations with...........................22
bottling up anger..................................37
breathe and relax...........................41, 60
brief vs. long exposure.........................57
CCCT utterances..................................27
celebrating your own choice................66
celebrations exercise............................68
chain of command................................23
changing topic......................................30
choice points.......................................115
cognitive therapy.................................45
Commands...27
communication, channels for...............92
competence..21
concentrate, rate, and concentrate.........88
consequences of options.....................107
contingent reinforcement.......................9
contradictions......................................27
coping rehearsal...................................58
criticism, responding to........................83
criticisms...28

cues, reading..92
curse words..34
deadlines..87
decision-making, steps.........................104
decisions...102
desensitization......................................57
disclosure of autistic status..................13
disrespectful talk..................................19
distinctness of speech...........................31
distressing behaviors............................18
disutility...108
down time..35
Dr. L.W. Aap, mnemonic....................110
dress, customs of..................................17
eccentricity...18
effort-payoff connection.........................9
Einstein..9
emotional climate.................................98
emotional climate, things to say, chart. .99
emotional regulation......................12, 37
emotions..38
employment, and life satisfaction...........9
enunciation...31
expected utility...................................108
exposure...57
expressing anger...................................19
eye contact...34
face, keeping distance from..................31
face, looking at.....................................34
facial expressions.................................94
facilitations..75
fantasy rehearsal............................49, 58
fear reduction, summary.......................64
fear, unwanted......................................54
feeling words.......................................39
fight or flight response.........................59

fingertip temperature..............................44
five important rules................................15
follow-up questions..............................76
four thought exercise.....................48, 61
four ways of listening..........................75
gestures..95
goals for mental health.......................68
good response to provocation.............38
good will meditation............................42
goofing off..35
greeting rituals.....................................24
guilt..38
habituation..57
happiness of self and others................68
hierarchy...56
homes for objects..................................88
honesty...67
hyperfocus...67
Ida Craft..51
ideas, organizing...................................91
individual decision..............................102
insults...19
internal sales pitch................................56
interrupting others' work......................32
interruptions..27
intimate zone...31
invitations..20
joint decision.......................................102
joint decision, example.......................112
joint decisions, tasks for.....................110
jokes...35
kind acts meditation.............................42
kindness to self and others meditation. .61
lateness...17
learning from the experience..............109
life satisfaction, and employment............9
listening responses...............................73
listing options.............................107, 111

long enough exposure...........................57
loudness..18
loudness of speech.................................30
loving kindness meditation...................42
mastery rehearsal...................................59
mastery vs. avoidance............................56
mature sources of power........................53
me too movement...................................20
measuring outcomes...............................21
meditation..42, 60
messages not to miss..............................96
mind-watching..60
Mozart..9
muscle relaxation...............................42, 60
names, learning and using......................33
Newton, Isaac...9
no-show..16
nonviolent options..................................50
OH RAM PRISM, mnemonic................62
one minute rule.................................26, 74
optimizing...103
options..107
options for provocations.........................50
organization skills...................................85
overcommitment......................................87
overdone negative thoughts....................47
overheard conversation...........................32
papers, organizing...................................89
parting rituals..24
PAST BAD, mnemonic...........................62
personal space...31
pitch differences in speech.....................93
positive emotional climate.....................98
positive feedback....................................76
power, sources of....................................51
priority score for to do list items...........86
prompts for reflections...........................78
provocation..38

psychological skills list............................69

pulse oximeter......................................44

questions about emotions......................40

raising the voice...................................37

reflecting..111

reflections...78

relaxation strategies.............................41

restricted range of interests..................66

revenge fantasies..................................18

rules for workplace...............................15

satisficing...103

self-discipline............................62, 109

self-talk.......................................45, 58

sensory aversions..................................12

sensory presentation.............................17

Shakespeare's plays..............................74

signal function of emotion.....................39

signals to stop talking...........................26

signals, reading.....................................92

smells..18

social conversation.........................12, 73

social conversation, example of............81

SOIL ADDLE, mnemonic...................109

staring...34

starting over...30

SUD level...55

supervisors, relations with....................22

sympathetic nervous system............41, 59

tact...28

talking too long....................................26

thoughts as influence on feelings..........44

threats...28

to do list...86

tones of approval exercises...................94

tones of voice.......................................92

topic changing......................................30

topic of conversation............................29

topics, dangerous and safe....................33

turn-taking in conversation.............26, 74

twelve thought exercise.........................47

twelve thought system..........................45

unwritten rules.....................................11

utility..108

utterances for emotional climate...........99

violence..18

workplace skills....................................11